Instant Pot Cookbook

250 Healthy, Easy and Quick-to-Make Instant Pot Pressure Cooker Recipes

Jessica Williams

Copyright © [Jessica Williams]

All rights reserved. No part of this guide may be reproduced in any form without permission in writing from the publisher except in the case of brief quotations embodied in critical articles or reviews.

Table of Contents

Table of Contents 3

Introduction 11

Chapter 1 Breakfast Recipes 12

Shakshuka 12

Eggs and Avocado Stir-Fry 12

Breakfast Casserole 13

Breakfast Quiche 13

Pumpkin Bread 14

Cheesy Breakfast Bagels 14

Quinoa and Bulgur Porridge 15

Savory Breakfast Grits 15

Fluffy Pancake 15

Banana Nut Oatmeal 16

Blueberry French Toast Casserole 16

French Toast Pudding 17

Miso Oat Porridge 17

Rice Pudding 18

Zucchini Frittata 18

Quinoa Breakfast Bowl 18

Potato Pancakes 19

Oats with Milk and Blueberry 19

Buckwheat Porridge 20

Creamy Wheat Cereal 20

Breakfast Shake 20

Bacon and Egg Bake 21

Bacon and Sausage Omelet 21

Chapter 2 Snacks and Appetizers 23

Garlic Brussels Sprouts 23

Lemon Radish 23

Boiled Peanuts 23

Deviled Eggs 24

Chive Salmon Bites 24

Bacon Cheese Muffins 25

Tofu Wraps 25

Spicy Edamame Snack 26

Spring Rolls 26
Garlic Toast 27
Herbed Tomato 27
BBQ Cauliflower Florets 27
Green Croquettes 28
Spicy Cauliflower and Tomatoes 28
Deviled Egg Salad 29
Shrimp Salad 29
Cinnamon Carrots 30
Muffins 30
Cauliflower Mac and Cheese 30
Egg & Cheese Salad 31
Fingerling Potatoes with Herbs 31
Artichoke Dip 32
Corn on the Cob with Chips 32

Chapter 3 Pasta and Side Dishes 33

Balsamic Pasta Salad 33
Tuna Pasta and Cherry Tomatoes 33
Tuscan Pasta 34
Chicken Enchilada Pasta 34
Chicken Pasta 35
Arrabiatta Pasta 35
Italian Pasta Bolognese 36
Creamed Ziti with Mozzarella 36
Onion Penne Pasta 37
Mushroom Zucchini Pasta 37
Spinach Pasta 38
Minestrone Pasta Soup 38
Lemon Artichoke 38
Casserole 39
Cheesy Broccoli 39
Zesty Brussels Sprouts 40
Steamed Artichokes 40
Cheesy Spinach 40
Spinach Celery Stew 41
Cabbage Stew 42

Lemon Potatoes...42

Mashed Potato 43

Sweet Potato Mash 43

Butter Corn..43

Tender Sweet Peppers 44

Chapter 4 Rice, Grains, Beans... 45

Polenta...45

Proso Millet 45

Basmati Ragu 45

Oatmeal with Onions 46

Teff in Tomato Paste 46

Bean and Rice Casserole 47

Rosemary Creamed Polenta...47

Shrimp Risotto 47

Spinach Vermouth Risotto...48

Tomato Risotto 48

Baked Beans 49

Black Beans 49

Red Kidney Beans Burrito 50

Cowboy Caviar..50

Creamy Kidney Beans 51

Green Bean and Lentil Stew 51

Biryani Rice 52

Potato and Green Bean Salad 52

Green Chili Baked Beans..53

Refried Pinto Beans 53

Chickpea Basil Salad 54

Cilantro Lime Brown Rice..54

Chapter 5 Soups and Stews 55

Lamb Stew...55

Rabbit Cabbage Stew 55

Pork Meatball Stew 56

Worcestershire Chili 56

Spiced Chili 57

Italian Sausage and Kale Soup..57

Broccoli and Cauliflower Soup..58

Italian Chicken Soup 58

Butternut Squash Soup 58

Hearty Hamburger Soup 59

Pumpkin and Bacon Soup 59

Clam Chowder 60

Mexican Soup 60

Cheesy Pepper Soup 61

Cheddar Chicken Soup 62

Beef Cabbage Soup 62

Summer Vegetable Soup 62

Creamy Tomato Basil Soup 63

Split Pea Soup 64

Sweet Potato Stew.. 64

White Bean & Swiss Chard Stew 65

Butternut Quinoa Chili 65

Curried Squash Soup 66

Chapter 6 Vegetable Recipes 67

Minestrone Soup 67

Chipotle Sweet Potato Chowder 67

Taco Soup 68

Beans with Jalapenos 68

Lemon Ginger Asparagus 69

Slaw in Cups 69

Creamy Corn 70

Cauliflower Veggie Mashup 70

Red Thai Curry Cauliflower 71

Butternut Mac 'N' Cheese 71

Broccoli Patties 72

Sweet Potato Burgers 72

Black Bean Burger 73

Seitan Burger 73

Apple Patties 74

Zucchini Patties 74

Pumpkin Burger 75

Pumpkin Cream Soup 75

Cauliflower Soup 76

French Onion Soup 76
Lentil Soup 77
Vegetable Stew 77
Peas and Carrot Stew 78
Sweet Potato Stew II 78
Turkish Green Beans 79
Lentil Gumbo 79

Chapter 7 Poultry Recipes 80

Kung Pao Chicken 80
Chicken Cacciatore 80
Chicken Casserole 81
Spicy Turkey Meatballs 81
Salsa Verde Chicken 82
Italian Duck with Spinach 82
Soft and Juicy Chicken 83
Chicken Bowl with Pine Nuts 83
Greek Chicken and Rice 84
Turkey Cheese Gnocchi 84
Chicken with Smoked Paprika 85
Turkey Noodle Soup 86
Duck Breast with Prosciutto 86
Salsa Verde Turkey Breast 87
Italian Chicken Thighs 88
Glazed Duck Breast 88
Chicken and Corn Soup 89
Chicken and Pea Soup 89
Chicken and Rice Soup 90
Turkey Salad 90
Turkey and Eggplant Mix 90
Lemongrass Turkey 91
Duck Curry 91
Parmesan Duck Breast 92
Duck and Rice Mix 92
Duck and Lentils 92

Chapter 8 Pork Recipes 94

Chinese Pork Soup 94

Pork Chops 94
Cinnamon Pork 95
Ginger Pork 95
Chinese Pulled Pork 96
Pork Chops with Peppers 96
Green Beans with Pork and Potatoes 97
Coffee Flavored Pork Ribs 97
Pork and Fennel Soup 97
Cinnamon Pork Stew 98
Sweet Potato and Pork Stew 98
Sage Pork Stew 99
Pork Bites 99
Pork Chops with Apples 99
Tomato Pork Chops 100
Sesame Pork Chops 100
Pork Chops and Cauliflower Rice 100
Rosemary Pork and Green Beans 101
Mustard Pork Ribs 101
Oregano and Spring Onion Pork 102
Pork Chops and Bell Peppers 102
Pork, Corn and Green Beans 102
Pork Shoulder and Celery 103
Pork, Spinach and Dill 103
Pork and Ginger Broccoli 103
Tarragon Pork Mix 104

Chapter 9 Beef and Lamb Recipes 105

Spicy Lamb 105
Lamb Curry with Zucchini 105
Cheesy Cajun Beef 106
Balsamic Fried Beef Roast 106
Beef Stroganoff 107
Classic Beef Stew 107
Traditional Goulash 108
Mushroom Burgers 108
Steak and Cauliflower Rice 109
Balsamic Beef 109

Lamb with Tomatoes 110

Picadillo..110

Grilled Beef Tenderloin... 111

Beef Stew 111

Rosemary Lamb 112

Lamb Stew with Bacon..112

Greek Lamb Stew 113

Lamb Ribs 113

Lamb Chops 114

Beef and Lamb Mix 114

Chapter 10 Fish and Seafood Recipes... 115

Salmon with Vegetables 115

Simple Crab Legs 115

Crab Bisque 115

Salmon with Broccoli 116

Cajun Shrimp with Asparagus 116

Dijon Halibut 117

Sockeye Salmon...117

Shrimp Zoodles 117

Steamed Tuna Steaks 118

Shrimp with Tomatoes and Feta..118

Clam Chowder II 119

Salmon with Green Beans 120

Sea Bass with Vegetables 120

Fish Bowls...121

Trout and Capers Sauce 121

Lemon Cod and Scallions...121

Cod and Cauliflower Rice 122

Spicy Trout 122

Salmon Cakes and Sauce.. 122

Cod and Strawberries Sauce 123

Chapter 11 Desserts..124

Mint Chocolate Chip Ice Cream... 124

Ice Cream Bites 124

Mini Chocolate Cakes 125

Classic Brownies.. 125

Easy Pecan Cookie Bars 126
Coconut Cookie Bites 126
Pound Cake 127
Chocolate Brownies 127
Almond Butter Cookies 128
Eggnog 128
Cherry Pudding 129
Chocolate Bundt Cake 129
Strawberry Cake 130
Creamy Raspberry Cake 130
Ruby Pears 131
Lemon Marmalade 131
Berry Jam 132
Pear Jam 132
Carrot Cake II 132
Raisin Pudding 133

Conclusion 134

Introduction

Eating healthy gets much easier with this delicious collection of Instant Pot recipes. This Instant Pot cookbook makes it easier and tastier for beginner Instant Pot users who love to eat a real homemade meal daily. This cooking appliance cuts down cooking time without sacrificing the delicious taste of the foods. Cooking has become easier after the invention of this great cooking device – the Instant Pot. Whether you are a skilled cook or a novice, the Instant Pot opens up a world of possibilities when cooking.

This Instant Pot cookbook was developed by a seasoned cook for maximum health and flavor. In this cookbook, you will find flavorful, nutritious, simple yet mouthwatering Instant Pot recipes. Every single recipe comes with detailed directions and a complete ingredients list that will leave you with no excuses not to cook a perfect meal and to look forward to enjoying its delicious taste. Meticulously planned, rich, and delicious recipes in this book ensure that there are no leftovers, no waste, and no guesswork, which is important for a beginner like you.

Next time you cook for your family members, partner, friends, or whomever, they will absolutely love these meals. This guide is your ultimate guide to Instant Pot cooking. This cookbook will not only let you know all the important facts about cooking but also will show you 500 easy Instant Pot recipes. Recipes include breakfasts, snacks, appetizers, pasta, side dishes, rice, grains, beans, soups, stews, vegetables, poultry, pork, beef, lamb, fish, seafood and desserts. If you do not own an Instant Pot now, then the recipes in this cookbook will definitely convince you to get one. Click "Buy Now" to purchase this book and start your new life!

Chapter 1 Breakfast Recipes

Shakshuka
Cook time: 15 minutes | Serves: 6 | Per serving: Calories 504; Carbs 7g; Fat 39g; Protein 29g

Ingredients:

- Ground chorizo – 1 pound
- Eggs – 6
- Cumin – ½ tbsp.
- Diced onion – ½ cup
- Red bell pepper – 1, diced
- Canned diced tomatoes – 28 ounces
- Minced garlic – 1 tsp.
- Coconut oil – 1 tsp.
- Pepper – ¼ tsp.
- Salt – ½ tsp.
- Water – 1 ½ cup

Directions:

Press Sauté and melt the coconut oil in it. Add the onions and peppers and sauté for 3 minutes. Add garlic and cook for 30 seconds more. Add chorizo and cook until browned. Stir in the tomatoes. Transfer the mixture to a baking dish. Clean and pour the water into the instant pot and lower the rack. Crack the eggs into the baking dish and place it on the rack. Close the lid and cook on High for 10 minutes. Serve.

Eggs and Avocado Stir-Fry
Cook time: 10 minutes | Serves: 2 | Per serving: Calories 350; Carbs 2.6g; Fat 32.7g; Protein 8.4g

Ingredients:

- Medium avocado – 1, pitted and cubed
- Eggs – 2 large, beaten
- Green onions – 2 tbsps. finely chopped
- Olive oil – 1 tsp.
- Butter – 1 tbsp.
- Sea salt – ½ tsp.
- Black pepper – ¼ tsp. ground
- Red chili flakes – ¼ tsp.

Directions:

Melt the butter in the instant pot. Press the Sauté button and add avocado cubes. Season with salt and pepper and cook for 3 to 4 minutes. Stirring occasionally. Now, add the green onions, eggs, and olive oil to taste. Add 2 tbsps. of milk for a creamier texture. Cook until the eggs are set, about 3 minutes. Transfer the dish to the serving plate. Top with heavy cream and serve.

Breakfast Casserole

Cook time: 15 minutes |Serves: 6| Per serving: Calories 484; Carbs 4.2g; Fat 38.9g; Protein 26.1g

Ingredients:

- Olive oil – 1 tbsp.
- Broccoli – 1 medium, chopped
- Pork sausages – 12 oz. cooked and cut into inch slices
- Cheddar cheese – 1 cup, grated
- Eggs – 10
- Salt – ½ tsp.
- Whipping cream – ¾ cup
- Garlic – 2 cloves, minced
- Ground black pepper – ¼ tsp.

Directions:

Grease the inside the instant pot with olive oil. Layer half of the broccoli, then half of the sausages and half of the cheese. Repeat with the rest of the ingredients. In a bowl, whisk the eggs and salt. Add the cream, garlic, and pepper. Whisk well. Pour the mixture over the ingredients in the instant pot. Cover and cook 15 minutes on High. Serve.

Breakfast Quiche

Cook time: 20 minutes |Serves: 6| Per serving: Calories 178; Carbs 3.8g; Fat 11.2g; Protein 15.3g

Ingredients:

- Diced tomatoes – 1 cup
- Chopped spinach – 3 cups
- Grated Parmesan cheese – ¼ cup
- Milk – ½ cup
- Green onions – 3, chopped
- Eggs – 12
- Tomato – ½, sliced
- Garlic salt – ½ tsp.
- Pepper – ¼ tsp.
- Water – 1 ½ cups

Directions:

Pour the water into the instant pot. Grease the baking dish with cooking spray. Combine the spinach, green onions, and diced tomatoes in it. Beat the eggs along with milk, salt, and pepper. Pour the mixture over the tomatoes and spinach. Sprinkle with parmesan cheese and top with tomato slices. Place the baking dish on the rack and close the lid. Cook on High for 20 minutes. Serve.

Pumpkin Bread

Cook time: 25 minutes| Serves: 4| Per serving: Calories 275; Carbs 5.8g; Fat 21.8g; Protein 10.7g

Ingredients:

- Pumpkin puree – ½ cup
- Large eggs – 2, beaten
- Almond flour – 1 cup
- Almond milk – ¼ cup
- Almond butter – 1 tbsp. melted
- Salt – ½ tsp.
- Nutmeg – ¼ tsp. ground
- Pumpkin pie spice – ½ tsp.
- Turmeric powder – ¼ tsp.

Directions:

In a bowl, combine the flour, pumpkin pie spice, turmeric, nutmeg, salt, and baking powder. Stir until combined and add eggs, milk, and pumpkin puree. Mix well and set aside. Grease a springform pan with melted butter. Add the dough and cover with aluminum foil. Pour 1 cup of water and place a trivet on the bottom and place the pan on top. Cover the pot and cook 25 minutes on Low. Cool completely. Slice and serve.

Cheesy Breakfast Bagels

Cook time: 15 minutes |Serves: 3| Per serving: Calories 367; Carbs 3.5g; Fat 29g; Protein 20g

Ingredients:

- Almond flour – ¾ cup
- Mozzarella cheese – 1 ½ cups, grated and melted
- Egg – 1
- Cream cheese – 2 tbsps.
- Xanthan gum – 1 tsp.
- Pinch of sea salt
- Water – 1 ½ cups
- Butter – 1 tbsp. melted

Directions:

Pour the water into the Instant Pot and place in a trivet. Beat the egg along with xanthan gum and salt. Whisk in the cheeses. Stir in the flour. Form a log out of the dough and divide it into three equal pieces. Make three bagel shape rings and flatten them. Brush with the butter. Arrange on a greased baking tray and place on the trivet. Cover and cook on Manual for 15 minutes. Serve.

Quinoa and Bulgur Porridge

Cook time: 6 minutes |Serves: 5| Per serving: Calories 349; Carbs 46.2g; Fat 11.9g; Protein 14.5g

Ingredients:

- Coconut milk – 3 cups, unsweetened
- Water – 1 cup
- Chia seeds – 3 tbsps.
- Quinoa – 1 cup, rinsed and drained
- Bulgur – ½ cup
- Grated nutmeg – 1 pinch
- Sea salt – 1 pinch
- Ground cardamom – ½ tsp.
- Ground anise – ½ tsp.
- Ground cloves – ¼ tsp.
- Black currants – ½ cup
- Honey for serving

Directions:

Add everything in the Instant Pot, except for the honey. Cover and cook on High for 6 minutes. Do a natural release and open. Serve with honey.

Savory Breakfast Grits

Cook time: 15 minutes |Serves: 6| Per serving: Calories 184; Carbs 6.2g ; Fat 15g ; Protein 6.5g

Ingredients:

- Milk – 1 cup
- Water – 2 ½ cups
- Cheddar cheese – 1 cup, shredded
- Olive oil – 2 Tbsps.
- Grits – 1 cup

Directions:

Pour two cups of water into the Instant Pot and place in a trivet. In a bowl, mix 2 tbsps. Of olive oil, the rest of the water, and grits. Cover the bowl with aluminum foil. Place the bowl on top of the trivet. Close the lid. Cook on High for 15 minutes. Then do a quick release. Remove the bowl from the Instant Pot and transfer the grit mixture to a large bowl. Add cheese and milk to the grit mixture and stir until the cheese has melted. Serve.

Fluffy Pancake

Cook time:17 minutes |Serves: 2| Per serving: Calories 480; Carbs 74.1 g ; Fat 14.7g ; Protein 14.3g

Ingredients:

- Egg – 1
- Olive oil – 1 ½ tbsps.

- Buttermilk – 1 ¼ cups
- Baking soda – ¾ tsp.
- Baking powder – ¾ tsp.
- Brown sugar – 3 tbsps.
- All-purpose flour – 1 cup

Directions:

Mix the flour, baking soda, baking powder, and sugar in a bowl. Add oil, buttermilk, and eggs and whisk until mixed. Spray a springform pan with cooking spray. Pour batter into the prepared pan. Pour 1 cup of water into the Instant Pot and place in a trivet. Place the pan on top of the trivet. Cover and cook on Low for 17 minutes. Do a natural release and open the lid. Slice and serve.

Banana Nut Oatmeal

Cook time: 3 minutes |Serves: 2| Per serving: Calories 218; Carbs 28.8g ; Fat 8g ; Protein 8.9g

Ingredients:

- Banana – 1, chopped
- Walnuts – ¼ cup, chopped
- Honey – 1 tsp.
- Milk – 2 cups
- Water – 2 cups
- Steel-cut oats – 1 cup

Directions:

Add water, milk, and oats to the Instant Pot and mix well. Cover and then cook on High for three minutes. Do a natural release and open the lid. Add walnuts, banana, and honey to the oats and stir well. Serve.

Blueberry French Toast Casserole

Cook time: 25 minutes |Serves: 4| Per serving: Calories 212; Carbs 35.7g ; Fat 4.2g ; Protein 8.8g

Ingredients:

- French bread slices – 4, cut into pieces
- Blueberries – 1 cup
- Cinnamon – ½ tsp.
- Vanilla – ½ tsp.
- Brown sugar – ¼ cup
- Eggs – 2
- Milk – 1 cup

Directions:

In a bowl, whisk eggs with vanilla, cinnamon, sugar, and milk. Add bread pieces and blueberries and mix to coat well. Spray baking dish with cooking spray. Pour mixture into the baking dish.

Pour ¾ cup of water into the Instant Pot and place a trivet in the pot. Place baking dish on top of the trivet and close the lid. Cook on High for 25 minutes. Do a natural release. Open and serve.

French Toast Pudding

Cook time: 16 minutes |Serves: 5 |Per serving: Calories 387; Carbs 59.6 g ; Fat 14.5g ; Protein 8.9g

Ingredients:

- Bananas – 4, chopped
- Almond milk – 1 cup
- Vegan French bread – 4 slices
- Maple syrup – 2 tbsps.
- Vanilla extract – 1 tsp
- Vegan butter – 1 tbsp.
- Ground cinnamon – 1 tsp.
- Ground cloves – ¼ tsp.
- Water – 1 cup, for cooking

Directions:

Pour water into the Instant Pot. Chop the bread and place it in a round pan. Blend together the maple syrup, chopped bananas, vanilla extract, ground cinnamon, and ground cloves until smooth. Pour the mixture over the bread. Cover the pan with the foil and secure the edges well. Place the pan in the IP. Close the lid and cook on High for 16 minutes. Do a quick release. Open the lid and remove the foil. Add the butter and stir gently. Serve.

Miso Oat Porridge

Cook time: 4 minutes |Serves: 4| Per serving: Calories 394 ; Carbs 16.9 g ; Fat 36g ; Protein 5.7g

Ingredients:

- Steel-cut oats – 1 cup
- Miso paste – 1 tsp.
- Tahini - 1 tbsp.
- Avocado – ½, peeled
- Nutritional yeast – ½ tsp.
- Almond milk – 2 cups
- Chives – ½ tsp. chopped

Directions:

Mix together the almond milk, nutritional yeast, and tahini. Then pour the mixture into the Instant Pot. Add the oats and stir gently. Close the lid. Cook the oats on High for 4 minutes. Do natural pressure. Meanwhile, mash the avocado well. Add miso paste and chives. Stir until smooth. Transfer the cooked oats in a bowl and add avocado mash. Stir and serve.

Rice Pudding

Cook time: 8 minutes |Serves:4 | Per serving: Calories 376; Carbs 81.1g ; Fat 2g ; Protein 5.5g

Ingredients:

- Rice - 1 ½ cups
- Rice milk – 3 cups
- All-purpose flour – 1 tbsp.
- Brown sugar – 2 tbsps.
- Turmeric – ¼ tsp.
- Vanilla extract – 1 tsp.

Directions:

In a bowl, combine ½-cup rice milk and flour. Add sugar, turmeric, and vanilla extract. Then pour it in the Instant Pot bowl. Add rice, and remaining milk. Stir to mix. Close and cook on High for 8 minutes. Do a natural release. Open the lid and stir. Serve.

Zucchini Frittata

Cook time:12 minutes |Serves: 5| Per serving: Calories 83; Carbs 7.3g ; Fat 4.9g ; Protein 4.1g

Ingredients:

- Firm tofu – 6 oz.
- Zucchini – 1
- Red onion – 1, diced
- Almond milk – ¼ cup
- Salt – 1 tsp.
- Ground black pepper – 1 tsp.
- Wheat flour – 2 tbsps.
- Olive oil – ½ tsp.

Directions:

Grate zucchini and scrambled tofu. Mix up together zucchini, tofu, onion, and almond milk. Add salt, ground black pepper, and wheat flour. Mix well. Brush the Instant Pot bowl with olive oil. Transfer the zucchini mixture into it. Flatten with a spatula. Close and cook 12 minutes on High pressure. Do a natural release. Open and serve.

Quinoa Breakfast Bowl

Cook time: 14minutes |Serves: 3| Per serving: Calories 459; Carbs 30.8g ; Fat 35.4g ; Protein 8.8g

Ingredients:

- Quinoa – ½ cup, soaked
- Almond milk – 1 ½ cups
- Coconut shredded – 1 tbsp.

- Maple syrup – 2 tsps.
- Vanilla extract – 1 tsp.
- Ground cinnamon – ½ tsp.
- Hemp seeds – 1 tbsp.

Directions:

Place quinoa and almond milk in the Instant Pot bowl. Add vanilla extract and stir gently. Close the lid and press Rice. Cook quinoa for 14 minutes on Low. Then transfer cooked quinoa in a bowl and add maple syrup, coconut shred, and ground cinnamon. Add hemp seeds and mix the mixture well. Serve.

Potato Pancakes
Cook time: 15 minutes |Serves: 4| Per serving: Calories 159; Carbs 29g; Fat 3.7g ; Protein 3.2g

Ingredients:

- Potatoes – 3, peeled
- Wheat flour – 2 tbsps.
- Cornstarch – 1 tsp.
- Salt – 1 tsp.
- Ground black pepper – ½ tsp.
- Chives – 1 tbsp.
- Fresh dill – 1 tsp. chopped
- Olive oil – 1 tbsp.

Directions:

Grate potatoes and mix them up with wheat flour, cornstarch, salt, black pepper, chives, and fresh dill. Separate the mixture into 4 parts. Preheat the Instant Pot and add olive oil. Place the first part of the potato mixture in the Instant pot and then flatten it to make the shape of a pancake. Cook on Sauté for 4 minutes on each side. Repeat and serve.

Oats with Milk and Blueberry
Cook time: 10 minutes |Serves: 4| Per serving: Calories 328; Carbs 47g ; Fat 13g ; Protein 10g

Ingredients:

- Steel-cut oats – 2 cups
- Water – 4 ½ cups
- Non-dairy milk – 1 cup
- Agave or maple syrup – 2 tbsps.
- Salt – ¼ tsp.
- Chia seeds – ¼ to ½ cup
- Chopped walnuts – 1 cup
- Fresh blueberries – 1 cup

Directions:

In the Instant Pot, stir together the water and oats. Cover and cook on High for 10 minutes. Open and add the milk. Stir in agave and salt. Top with blueberries, walnuts, and chia seeds and serve.

Buckwheat Porridge

Cook time: 3 minutes |Serves: 2| Per serving: Calories 438; Carbs 51g ; Fat 28g ; Protein 6.2g

Ingredients:

- Raw buckwheat – 1 cup
- Coconut milk – 3 cups, divided
- Banana – 1
- Dried cranberries – ¼ cup
- Splash of vanilla
- Dash of cinnamon

Directions:

Add everything in the Instant Pot and cover. Cook on High for 3 minutes. Open and add another splash of milk. Stir to thicken. Serve.

Creamy Wheat Cereal

Cook time: 2 minutes |Serves: 2| Per serving: Calories 538; Carbs 58g; Fat 32g ; Protein 12g

Ingredients:

- Ground wheat berries – 2 cups
- Agave nectar – 1 tbsp.
- Coconut milk – 2 cups
- Splash of vanilla
- Cocoa powder – 1 tbsp.

Directions:

In the Instant Pot, add everything and mix. Cover and cook on High for 2 minutes. Do a natural release. Serve.

Breakfast Shake

Cook time: 5 minutes| Serves: 3| Per serving: Calories 333; Carbs 8g; Fat 26g ; Protein 18g

Ingredients:

- Butter – 2 tbsps. softened
- Full-fat coconut milk – ½ cup
- Liquid stevia – 10 drops
- Pecans – 1 tbsp. chopped
- Cashews – 1 tbsp. chopped

- Macadamia nuts – 1 tbsp. chopped
- Cinnamon – ½ tsp. ground
- Turmeric – ½ tsp. ground
- Heavy whipping cream – ¼ cup
- Mixed dark berries – ¼ cup
- Whey protein powder – 2 scoops
- Ice cubes to serve
- Water – 1 ½ cups

Directions:

Pour 1 ½ cups of water into a blender. Press sauté on the Instant Pot and melt the butter. Pour in the coconut milk. Then add the berries, whipping cream, turmeric, cinnamon, macadamia nuts, cashews, pecans, and stevia. Stir continuously. Press Cancel when mixed well. Pour the mixture into the blender. Add the protein powder and blend well. Serve with ice.

Bacon and Egg Bake
Cook time: 19 minutes |Serves: 3| Per serving: Calories 302; Carbs 4.5g ; Fat 23.9g ; Protein 17.6g

Ingredients:

- Eggs – 5
- Bacon – 3 slices, cooked and finely chopped
- Avocado oil – 2 tbsps.
- Kale – ½ cup, chopped
- Broccoli – ½ cup, chopped
- Heavy whipping cream – ½ cup
- Cayenne pepper – ½ tsp. ground
- Basil – ½ tsp. dried
- Kosher salt and pepper to taste
- Water – 1 cup

Directions:

Add 1-cup of water into the Instant Pot and place in the trivet. In a bowl, combine basil, salt, black pepper, cayenne pepper, whipping cream, broccoli, kale, oil, bacon, and eggs. Mix well. Place in a dish and cover with foil. Place on top of the trivet. Close and cook 19 minutes on High. Do a natural release and open. Serve.

Bacon and Sausage Omelet
Cook time:25 minutes |Serves: 6| Per serving: Calories 222; Carbs 3.5g ; Fat 15g ; Protein 16g

Ingredients:

- Eggs – 6
- Bacon slices – 6, cooked and crumbled

- Sausage links – 6, sliced
- Onions – 1, diced
- Almond milk – ½ cup
- Garlic powder – ¼ tsp.
- Salt – ¼ tsp.
- Pepper – ¼ tsp.
- Water – 1 ½ cups

Directions:

Pour the water into the Instant Pot and lower the rack. Beat the eggs along with the milk and seasonings. Add the remaining ingredients. Grease a baking dish with cooking spray. Pour the egg mixture into it. Place the dish on the rack and cover. Cook on Manual for 25 minutes. Serve.

Chapter 2 Snacks and Appetizers

Garlic Brussels Sprouts
Cook time:6 minutes |Serves: 4| Per serving: Calories 128; Carbs 6g ; Fat 8g ; Protein 4g

Ingredients:

- Minced garlic – 2 tsps.
- Brussels sprouts – 1 pound, trimmed, and halved
- Water – ½ cup
- Coconut oil – 2 tbsps.
- Chopped yellow onion – ½ cup
- Salt and black pepper to taste

Directions:

Press Sauté and add oil to the Instant Pot. Then add garlic and onions. Stir-fry for 2 minutes. Add the rest of the ingredients and mix. Cover and cook 2 minutes on High. Do a quick release and open the lid. Drain excess liquid and serve on a plate.

Lemon Radish
Cook time: 7 minutes| Serves: 4| Per serving: Calories 76; Carbs 4g ; Fat 5g; Protein 6g

Ingredients:

- Radishes – 2 cups, peeled and cut into rounds
- Chicken stock – ½ cup
- Melted ghee – 2 tbsps.
- Grated lemon zest – 1 tbsp.
- Salt and black pepper to taste
- Chopped chives – 1 tbsp.

Directions:

Add the radishes, with salt, pepper, stock, and lemon zest. Stir to mix well. Close and cook 8 minutes on High. Open the lid and add ghee and chives. Serve.

Boiled Peanuts
Cook time: 30 minutes |Serves: 8| Per serving: Calories 168; Carbs 11.1g ; Fat 10.6g ; Protein 7.5g

Ingredients:

- Green peanuts in shells – 2 cups
- Water – 2 cups
- Salt – 2 tsps.
- Cayenne pepper – 1 tsp.

- Taco seasoning – 1 tsp.

Directions:

Place green peanuts, water, salt, cayenne pepper, and taco seasoning in the Instant Pot. Close and cook on High for 30 minutes. Open and drain water and transfer peanuts into the serving bowl. Serve.

Deviled Eggs
Cook time: 6 minutes |Serves: 4| Per serving: Calories 132; Carbs 1g ; Fat 11g ; Protein 6g

Ingredients:

- Eggs – 4
- Mayonnaise – 2 tbsps.
- Olive oil – 1 tbsp.
- Dijon mustard – 1 tsp.
- Apple cider vinegar – ½ tsp.
- Sriracha – ¼ tsp.
- Paprika to taste
- Water – 1 cup for the pot

Directions:

Arrange a steamer basket in the bottom of the instant pot and add 1 cup water. Place eggs into the steamer basket. Cook on High for 6 minutes. Open and peel the eggs and cut in half lengthwise. Remove the yolks and transfer into a bowl. Mash the egg yolks with a fork. Except for paprika, add remaining ingredients and mix well. Fill the egg whites with this mixture. Sprinkle with paprika and serve.

Chive Salmon Bites
Cook time: 10 minutes |Serves: 4| Per serving: Calories 180; Carbs 7g ; Fat 3g ; Protein 9g

Ingredients:

- Lemon juice – 1 tbsp.
- Oil – 1 tbsp.
- Salmon fillets – 1 pound, skinless, boneless, and cubed
- Garlic – 2 cloves, minced
- Chives – 1 tbsp. chopped
- Lime zest – 1 tbsp. grated
- Water – 1 cup

Directions:

In a bowl, mix the salmon cubes with the rest of the ingredients except the chives and water and mix. Add the water and the steamer basket in the pot. Add the salmon on top of the steamer basket and cover. Cook on High for 10 minutes. Open and serve sprinkled with chives.

Bacon Cheese Muffins

Cook time: 8 minutes |Serves: 3| Per serving: Calories 170; Carbs 1g ; Fat 13g ; Protein 12g

Ingredients:

- Cheddar cheese – 4 tbsps. shredded
- Lemon pepper seasoning – ¼ tsp.
- Precooked bacon – 4 slices, crumbled
- Green onion – 1, diced
- Eggs – 4
- Water – 1 ½ cups for the pot

Directions:

Arrange the steamer basket inside the pot and add 1 ½ cups of water. Whisk the eggs in a bowl. Add the lemon pepper and beat again. Divide the bacon, green onion, and cheese into 4 muffin cups. Top with the egg mixture and stir to mix. Arrange the cups on the steamer basket. Cover and cook on High for 8 minutes. Serve.

Tofu Wraps

Cook time: 5 minutes| Serves: 6| Per serving: Calories 41; Carbs 2g ; Fat 2g ; Protein 3.6g

Ingredients:

- Lettuce leaves – 6
- Chili pepper – 1 tsp.
- Soy sauce – 1 tbsp.
- Brown sugar – 1 tsp.
- Water – 3 tbsps.
- Salt – ½ tsp.
- Firm tofu – 8 oz. chopped
- Mustard – 1 tsp.
- Olive oil – 1 tsp.
- Fresh parsley – 1 oz. chopped

Directions:

Make the tofu sauce: whisk together chili pepper, soy sauce, sugar, water, salt, mustard, and olive oil. Then combine together tofu and sauce. Let it marinate for 10 minutes. Press Sauté on the Instant Pot. Place the tofu and all marinade inside. Sauté and stir for 5 minutes. Remove the mixture from the IP and chill it until it reaches room temperature. Fill the lettuce leaves with chopped parsley and tofu. Sprinkle tofu wraps with the remaining cooked marinade and serve.

Spicy Edamame Snack

Cook time: 11 minutes | Serves: 6 | Per serving: Calories 89; Carbs 7.5g ; Fat 4g ; Protein 5.6g

Ingredients:

- Edamame beans – 1 cup
- Minced garlic – 1 tsp.
- Butter - 1 tbsp.
- Cayenne pepper – ½ tsp.
- Sesame seeds – 1 tbsp.
- Soy sauce – ¼ cup
- Salt – ¼ tsp.
- Brown sugar – ½ tsp.
- Water – 1 cup, for cooking

Directions:

Pour water into the Instant Pot. Add edamame beans and salt. Close and cook on High for 6 minutes. Meanwhile, mix minced garlic, cayenne pepper, sesame seeds, sugar, and soy sauce. Transfer cooked edamame beans in the bowl. Clean the pot and add butter and melt it on Sauté. Add soy sauce mixture and boil for 5 minutes. Chill the sauce. Pour the sauce over the edamame beans and mix. Serve.

Spring Rolls

Cook time: 4 minutes | Serves: 3 | Per serving: Calories 22; Carbs 4.5g ; Fat 0.2g ; Protein 2g

Ingredients:

- Red cabbage – ¼ cup, shredded
- Fresh parsley – 2 oz. chopped
- Mushrooms – 1 cup, chopped
- Carrot – 1 cut into wedges
- Soy sauce – 1 tbsp.
- Paprika – 1 tsp.
- Lemon juice – 1 tbsp.
- Lime zest – ¼ tsp.
- Chili flakes – ½ tsp.
- Spring roll wraps – 6
- Water – 1 cup, for cooking

Directions:

In a bowl, mix shredded red cabbage, fresh parsley, chopped mushrooms, carrot, soy sauce, paprika, lemon juice, lime zest, and chili flakes. Fill the spring roll wraps with the cabbage mixture. Wrap the spring roll wraps. Pour water in the Instant Pot and insert steamer rack inside. Place prepared spring rolls on the steamer rack. Close and cook on High for 4 minutes. Open and serve.

Garlic Toast

Cook time: 2 minutes |Serves: 2| Per serving: Calories 153; Carbs 17.7g ; Fat 8g ; Protein 3.1g

Ingredients:

- Bread slices – 4
- Minced garlic – 1 tbsp.
- Olive oil - 1 tbsp.

Directions:

Preheat the Instant Pot. Then add the olive oil. Add the bread slices and cook then on Sauté for 1 minute on each side. Remove the bread slices from the Instant Pot and rub with minced garlic from each side. Serve.

Herbed Tomato

Cook time: 20 minutes |Serves: 4| Per serving: Calories 30; Carbs 6.4g ; Fat 0.4g ; Protein 1.5g

Ingredients:

- Tomatoes – 4
- Fresh cilantro – 1 oz. chopped
- Garlic – 3 cloves, peeled
- Ground black pepper - 1 tsp.
- Salt - ½ tsp.
- Oregano – 1 tsp.
- Apple cider vinegar - 1 tbsp.
- Water – 1/3 cup

Directions:

Cut tomatoes into the halves and place them in the Instant Pot. Add fresh cilantro, garlic, ground black pepper, salt, oregano, apple cider vinegar, and water. Close the lid and cook on Sauté for 20 minutes. Stir it from time to time. Cool and serve.

BBQ Cauliflower Florets

Cook time:15 minutes| Serves:2 | Per serving: Calories 89; Carbs 15.8g ; Fat 2.9g ; Protein 1.3g

Ingredients:

- Cauliflower florets - 1 cup
- BBQ sauce – 4 tbsps.
- Turmeric – 1 tsp.
- Paprika – 1 tsp.
- Cayenne pepper – 1 tsp.
- Water – ¼ cup
- Olive oil - 1 tsp.

Directions:

Place cauliflower florets in a bowl. Add BBQ sauce, turmeric, paprika, cayenne pepper, water, and olive oil. Mix and set aside for 10 to 15 minutes to marinate. Then transfer it in the Instant Pot, add all the remaining BBQ sauce mixture. Sauté the cauliflower for 10 to 15 minutes or until cooked. Serve.

Green Croquettes
Cook time: 5 minutes| Serves: 4| Per serving: Calories 155; Carbs 20.6 g ; Fat 6.8g ; Protein 4.4g

Ingredients:

- Sweet potatoes – 2, peeled, boiled
- Fresh spinach – 1 cup
- Peanuts – 1 tbsp.
- Flax meal – 3 tbsps.
- Salt – 1 tsp.
- Ground black pepper – 1 tsp.
- Olive oil – 1 tbsp.
- Dried oregano – ½ tsp.
- Wheat flour – ¾ cup

Directions:

Mash the sweet potatoes and place them in a bowl. Add flax meal, salt, dried oregano, and ground black pepper. Then blend the spinach with peanuts until smooth. Add the green mixture in the sweet potato. Mix. Make medium size croquettes and coat them in the wheat flour. Preheat Instant Pot on Sauté mode well. Add olive oil. Roast croquettes for 1 minute on each side or until golden brown. Serve.

Spicy Cauliflower and Tomatoes
Cook time: 7 minutes |Serves: 4| Per serving: Calories 74; Carbs 3.3g ; Fat 1.7g ; Protein 4.5g

Ingredients:

- Chopped tomatoes – 2
- Chopped small onion – ½
- Green chile – 1
- Olive oil – 1 tsp.
- Ground cumin – 1 tsp.
- Ground turmeric – ½ tsp.
- Paprika – ½ tsp.
- Salt and black pepper to taste
- Cauliflower head – 1, cut into small florets
- Water – ½ cup
- Chopped fresh cilantro – 1 tbsp.

Directions:

Add onion, tomato, and green chile in a food processor and pulse until smooth. Add oil in the Instant Pot and press Sauté. Then add the pureed onion mixture and cook for 2 to 3 minutes. Add the spices and cook for 1 minute. Stir in cauliflower and water. Cover and cook on Low for 3 minutes. Serve.

Deviled Egg Salad

Cook time: 12 minutes| Serves: 5| Per serving: Calories 313; Carbs 1.3g ; Fat 26g ; Protein 16g

Ingredients:

- Eggs – 10
- Raw bacon – 5 strips
- Mayonnaise – 2 tbsps.
- Dijon mustard – 1 tsp.
- Smoked paprika – ¼ tsp.
- Green onion – 1 stalk
- Salt and pepper to taste

Directions:

Grease a cake pan that fits inside the IP. Add the raw eggs in the cake pan. Pour 1 cup of water into the bottom of the IP. Then place the steam rack, and place the cake pan on top of it. Cook on High for 6 minutes. Remove the cake pan and flip the pan to remove the egg loaf from the pan. Chop up the loaf and place in a bowl. Clean the inner bowl and place it again into the IP. Add chopped bacon, press Sauté and cook until crispy. Add the bacon and the fat to the chopped eggs. Add smoked paprika, mustard, mayonnaise and season with salt and pepper. Mix, garnish with chopped green onion. Serve.

Shrimp Salad

Cook time: 6 minutes |Serves: 4| Per serving: Calories 170; Carbs 7g ; Fat 9g ; Protein 6g

Ingredients:

- Shrimp – 1 pound, peeled and deveined
- Baby arugula – 2 cups
- Balsamic vinegar – 1 tbsp.
- Tomato paste – 2 tbsps.
- Spring onions – 2, chopped
- Oil – ½ tsp.
- Chili powder – ½ tsp.
- Oregano – ½ tsp. chopped
- Garlic – ½ tsp. minced

Directions:

Heat oil on Sauté. Add onions and cook for 2 minutes. Add the rest of the ingredients except the arugula and the vinegar. Cover and cook on High for 4 minutes. Open and transfer the shrimp mixture to a bowl. Add the arugula and vinegar. Mix and serve.

Cinnamon Carrots

Cook time: 4 minutes| Serves: 6 | Per serving: Calories 98; Carbs 3g ; Fat 8g ; Protein 4g

Ingredients:

- Erythritol – 2 tbsps. powdered
- Cinnamon – ½ tsp. ground
- Baby carrots – 2 pounds, trimmed
- Butter – 1/3 cup
- Salt to taste
- Water – ½ cup

Directions:

Add all the ingredients and mix well. Close and cook 4 minutes on High. Open and serve.

Muffins

Cook time: 8 minutes |Serves: 3| Per serving: Calories 170 ; Carbs 1g ; Fat 13g ; Protein 12g

Ingredients:

- Cheddar cheese – 4 tbsps. shredded
- Lemon pepper seasoning – ¼ tsp.
- Precooked bacon – 4 slices, crumbled
- Green onion – 1, diced
- Eggs – 4

Directions:

Arrange the steamer basket inside the pot and add 1 ½ cups of water. Whisk the eggs in a bowl. Add the lemon pepper and beat again. Divide the bacon, green onion, and cheese into 4 muffin cups. Top with the egg mixture and stir to mix. Arrange the cups on the steamer basket. Cover and cook for 8 minutes. Serve.

Cauliflower Mac and Cheese

Cook time: 5 minutes| Serves: 4| Per serving: Calories 134; Carbs 3g; Fat 11g ; Protein 6g

Ingredients:

- Cauliflower rice – 2 cups
- Cream cheese – 2 tbsps.
- Half-and-half – ½ cup
- Grated sharp cheddar cheese – ½ cup
- Salt and ground black pepper to taste

Directions:

In a bowl, mix the cheddar cheese, cauliflower, half-and-half, cream cheese, salt, and pepper. Cover the bowl with aluminum foil. Pour 2 cups of water into the Instant Pot and place a trivet in the Pot. Place the bowl on the trivet. Cover and cook on High for 5 minutes. Open and remove the bowl. Remove the foil. Place the cooked cauliflower under the broiler and broil for 3 to 5 minutes or until cheese is brown and bubbling. Serve.

Egg & Cheese Salad
Cook time: 5 minutes |Serves: 8| Per serving: Calories 113; Carbs 3.1g ; Fat 8.3g ; Protein 6.7g

Ingredients:

- Eggs – 8
- Grated hard cheese – 1 + ½ cups
- Garlic – 2 large cloves, grated
- Mayonnaise – 1/3 cup
- Yellow or Dijon mustard – 1 tsp.
- Pinch of salt
- Water – 1 cup for the pot

Directions:

Place a trivet on the bottom of the IP and add 1 cup of water. Place the eggs on top of the trivet. Cook for 5 minutes on High. Then open and remove the eggs and place them in cold water. To make the salad: peel and finely dice the eggs in a bowl. Reserve 1 egg yolk. Add the rest of the ingredients and mix well. Garnish with the egg yolk, fresh parsley, and black pepper. Serve.

Fingerling Potatoes with Herbs
Cook time: 19 minutes| Serves: 6| Per serving: Calories 391; Carbs 19.9g; Fat 35g; Protein 2.4g

Ingredients:

- Fingerling potatoes – 1 ½ pounds
- Thyme – 2 sprigs
- Rosemary – 2 sprigs
- Shallot powder – ½ tsp.
- Porcini powder – ½ tsp.
- Butter – 4 tbsps. melted
- Black pepper – ½ tsp.
- Cayenne pepper – ½ tsp.
- Garlic paste -1 tsp.
- Broth – ¾ cup
- Salt to taste

Directions:

Melt the butter on Sauté. Add the potatoes and sauté for 9 minutes. Then pierce the potatoes in the middle with a fork. Add everything and cover. Cook for 10 minutes on High. Serve.

Artichoke Dip
Cook time: 9 minutes| Serves: 8| Per serving: Calories 190; Carbs 10.3g; Fat 13.2g; Protein 1g

Ingredients:

- Ricotta cheese – 1 cup
- Romano cheese - 1 ¼ cups, grated
- Canned artichoke hearts – 12 ounces, chopped
- Garlic powder – 1 tsp.
- Shallot powder – ½ tsp.
- Gourmet mustard – 1 tsp.
- Salt and pepper to taste
- Cumin powder – ½ tsp.
- Kale – 2 cups, chopped
- Mayonnaise – ½ cup
- Water – 1 cup for the pot

Directions:

Grease a baking pan and add everything in it. Mix well. Add water and trivet to the pot. Pace the baking pan on top of the trivet and cover. Cook 9 minutes on High and serve.

Corn on the Cob with Chips
Cook time: 2 minutes |Serves: 4| Per serving: Calories 260; Carbs 52.5g; Fat 5.2g; Protein 5.7g

Ingredients:

- Barbecue sauce – 1/3 cup
- Corn on the cob – 4 ears, husks removed
- Potato chips – ½ cup, crushed
- Water – 1 cup for the pot

Directions:

Add water and a trivet to the pot. Place the corn on the trivet and cover. Cook on Steam for 2 minutes. Open and brush each corn with sauce and sprinkle with chips. Serve.

Chapter 3 Pasta and Side Dishes

Balsamic Pasta Salad

Cook time:10 minutes| Serves: 2 | Per serving: Calories 533; Carbs 79.8g; Fat 18.8g; Protein 15.1g

Ingredients:

- Extra virgin olive oil – 2 tbsps.
- Onion – 1, sliced
- Garlic – 2 tbsps. minced
- Corn – ½ cup, boiled
- Carrot – 1, chopped
- Olives – 6, without kernel
- Dried tomatoes – 2, chopped
- Pasta – ½ lb.
- Honey – 1 tsp.
- Mustard – 1 tsp.
- Balsamic vinegar – 1 tbsp.
- Salt and pepper to taste.

Directions:

Press Sauté on the Instant Pot and add oil. Add onion, salt, and sauté for 3 to 4 minutes. Add carrot, olives, corn, and tomatoes, and sauté for 2 minutes more. Add pasta and remaining ingredients and pour in the water. Season salt and pepper to taste and stir well. Cover the pot and cook on High for 4 minutes. Do a quick release. Open and serve.

Tuna Pasta and Cherry Tomatoes

Cook time:12 minutes| Serves: 4| Per serving: Calories 665; Carbs 79g; Fat 23g; Protein 37g

Ingredients:

- Tuna steaks – 8 ounces
- Penne pasta – 12 ounces
- Cherry tomatoes – 2 cups, halved
- Olives – 1/3 cup, pitted and halved
- Sweet onion – 1 cup, chopped
- Minced garlic – 2 tsps.
- Salt – ½ tsp.
- Ground black pepper – ½ tsp.
- Red chili flakes – ¼ tsp.
- Basil leaves – ½ cup, chopped
- Grated lemon zest – 1 ½ tsps.

- Lemon juice – 2 tbsps.
- Olive oil – 3 tbsps.
- Water – 2 ¾ cups

Directions:

Add onion, tomatoes, olives, garlic, red chili flakes, and pasta in the Instant Pot. Season with salt and black pepper and mix. Pour in water, stir to combine, then add tuna on top and cover. Cook on High for 6 minutes. Then do a quick release. Open and add remaining ingredients. Stir well and cover. Let pasta stand for 5 minutes, then serve.

Tuscan Pasta
Cook time: 10 minutes| Serves: 4| Per serving: Calories 322; Carbs 52.2g; Fat 7.6g; Protein 13g

Ingredients:

- Penne pasta – 8 ounces
- Bell pepper – 1, chopped
- Fresh spinach – 1 cup, chopped
- Onion – ½ chopped
- Broccoli florets – 1 cup
- Water – 2 cups
- Mozzarella – ½ cup, grated
- Tomato sauce – ½ cup
- Olive oil – 1 tbsp.
- Cremini mushrooms – 3 ½ ounces
- Parmesan cheese – 1 tbsp. grated
- Salt and pepper to taste

Directions:

Press Sauté and add oil in the Instant Pot. Add onion, mushroom, and bell pepper. Cook for 3 to 4 minutes. Add pasta, broccoli, spinach, tomato sauce, water, salt, and pepper. Cover the pot. Cook on High for 5 minutes. Do a quick release and open. Add mozzarella. Press Sauté and stir well until melted. Serve topped with parmesan cheese.

Chicken Enchilada Pasta
Cook time: 14 minutes| Serves: 6| Per serving: Calories 567; Carbs 49g; Fat 25g; Protein 31g

Ingredients:

- Chicken breast – 2, diced
- Dry pasta – 3 cups
- Canned tomatoes – 10 ounces
- Canned Enchilada sauce – 20 ounces
- Water – 1 ¼ cups

- Diced onion – 1 cup
- Garlic – 1 tsp. minced
- Taco seasoning – 1 tsp.
- Olive oil – 1 tbsp.
- Cheddar cheese – 2 cups, shredded

Directions:

Heat oil in the Instant Pot on Sauté. Add onions and cook for 3 minutes. Add the rest of the ingredients except for the cheese. Cover and cook on High for 8 minutes. Open and stir in cheese and cook for 2 minutes, lid off, on Sauté. Serve.

Chicken Pasta

Cook time: 12 minutes| Serves: 4| Per serving: Calories 510; Carbs 46.5g; Fat 17g; Protein 40.9g

Ingredients:

- Penne pasta – 8 oz. dry
- Chicken breast – 1 lb. boneless, skinless, chopped
- Fajita seasoning – 3 tbsps. divided into half
- Tomatoes – 7 oz., chopped
- Garlic – 4 cloves, minced
- Onion – 1, diced
- Chicken stock – 1 cup
- Bell peppers – 2, chopped
- Olive oil – 2 tbsps.

Directions:

Add olive oil in the Instant Pot and press Sauté. Add chicken and half fajita seasoning. Stir well and sauté until chicken looks white. Add garlic, bell pepper, onion, and remaining fajitas seasoning. Stir well and sauté for 2 minutes. Add tomatoes, stock, and pasta in the pot. Mix. Cover and cook on High for 6 minutes. Do a quick release, open, and serve.

Arrabiatta Pasta

Cook time:16 minutes| Serves: 3| Per serving: Calories 362; Carbs 62.4g; Fat 7.2g; Protein 11.7g

Ingredients:

- Italian seasoning – 1 tbsp.
- Minced garlic – 1 tsp.
- Tomato – 1, chopped
- Yellow onion – 3 oz. diced
- Pasta – 1 cup
- Water – 1 cup
- Pasta sauce – 1 cup

- Sesame oil – 1 tsp.

Directions:

Pour sesame oil in the Instant Pot. Press Sauté. Add minced garlic, chopped tomato, yellow onion, and sauté for 7 minutes. Add pasta sauce and water. Add pasta and cook on High for 7 minutes. Open and chill the cooked pasta for a few minutes and serve.

Italian Pasta Bolognese

Cook time: 25 minutes| Serves:4| Per serving: Calories 677; Carbs 43.3g; Fat 39.5g; Protein 43.3g

Ingredients:

- Penne rigate – 2 pounds
- Chopped jalapeno – 1
- Heavy cream – ¼ cup
- Garlic – 2 cloves, minced
- Celery – 1, diced small
- Sweet pepper – 1, finely chopped
- Broth – 1 ½ cups
- Italian tomatoes – 1 (28-ounce) can, chopped
- Leeks – 1 cup, chopped
- Olive oil -1 ½ tbsps.
- Ground pork – 1 pound
- Ground beef – ½ pound

Directions:

Add oil in the pot and cook leeks for 4 minutes on Sauté. Add garlic and cook for 1 minute more. Add ground meat and cook for 5 minutes. Add everything, except for the heavy cream. Cover and cook on High for 15 minutes. Open and stir in the cream. Serve.

Creamed Ziti with Mozzarella

Cook time: 10 minutes |Serves: 4| Per serving: Calories 459; Carbs 74.9g; Fat 8.2g; Protein 19.8g

Ingredients:

- Dry ziti pasta – 9 ounces
- Shredded mozzarella cheese – 1 cup
- Garlic – 2 cloves, minced
- Tomato sauce – 1 ½ cups
- Double cream – ½ cup
- Broth – 2 cups
- Salt and pepper to taste

Directions:

Add everything in the pot except for the mozzarella. Cover and cook on High for 8 minutes. Do a quick release and open. Add mozzarella and cover. Set aside until cheese melts. Serve.

Onion Penne Pasta

Cook time: 11 minutes |Serves: 6 | Per serving: Calories 264; Carbs 46g; Fat 2g; Protein 11g

Ingredients:

- Skimmed milk – 1 cup
- Small onion – 1, chopped
- Olive oil – 1 tsp.
- Water as needed
- Penne pasta – 12 ounces

Directions:

Add 3 cups water and pasta in the Instant Pot. Cover and cook on High for 6 minutes. Drain the pasta and transfer pasta in a bowl. Heat oil on Sauté and cook onions for 2 minutes. Add milk and cook for 3 minutes. Mix in pasta and serve.

Mushroom Zucchini Pasta

Cook time: 20 minutes| Serves: 5| Per serving: Calories 248; Carbs 12g; Fat 12.5g; Protein 3.5g

Ingredients:

- Mushrooms – 12, sliced
- Zucchini – 1, sliced
- Sherry wine – a few drops
- Shallot – 1, chopped
- Penne pasta – 15 ounces
- Tomato paste – 5 ounces
- Soy sauce – 2 tbsps.
- Yellow onion – 1, chopped
- Garlic – 2 cloves, minced
- Olive oil – 1 tbsp.
- Vegetable stock – 1 cup
- Water – 2 cups
- Basil – 1 pinch, dried
- Dried oregano – 1 pinch, dried
- Salt and black pepper to taste

Directions:

Add oil, onion, shallot, pepper, and salt and cook for 3 minutes on Sauté. Add garlic and cook 1 minute more. Add mushrooms, zucchini, basil, and oregano. Cook for 1 minute more. Mix in the stock, water, wine, and soy sauce. Add pasta and tomato sauce. Season and cover. Cook on High for 5 minutes. Open and serve.

Spinach Pasta

Cook time: 12 minutes| Serves: 3| Per serving: Calories 198; Carbs 26.5g; Fat 1g; Protein 7g

Ingredients:

- Garlic – 2 cloves, crushed
- Spinach – 1 pound
- Fusilli pasta – 1 pound
- Olive oil – 1 tbsp.
- Pine nuts – ¼ cup, chopped
- Salt and pepper to taste

Directions:

Add oil and cook garlic and spinach for 6 minutes on Sauté. Add pasta, salt, pepper and water to cover the pasta. Close and cook 6 minutes on High. Do a quick release open and add pine nuts. Serve.

Minestrone Pasta Soup

Cook time: 8 minutes| Serves: 2| Per serving: Calories 394; Carbs 58g; Fat 3g; Protein 20.5g

Ingredients:

- Chicken broth – 2 cups
- Elbow pasta – ½ cup
- Tomatoes – 14 ounces, diced
- Cooked white beans – 1 cup
- Carrot – 1, diced
- Dried basil – 1 tsp.
- Olive oil – 1 tbsp.
- Dried oregano – 1 tsp.
- Garlic – 2 cloves, minced
- Bay leaf – 1
- Onion – 1, diced
- Fresh spinach – ¼ cup
- Salt and pepper to taste

Directions:

Add oil in the instant pot. Cook carrot, onion, garlic, and celery for 5 minutes on Sauté. Add basil, oregano, pepper, salt and mix. Mix the spinach, tomatoes, broth, pasta and bay leaf. Close and cook on High for 6 minutes. Open and add the beans. Serve.

Lemon Artichoke

Cook time: 10 minutes| Serves: 4 | Per serving: Calories 142; Carbs 4g; Fat 12g; Protein 5g

Ingredients:

- Bone broth – 2 cups
- Tarragon leaves – 1 tbsp.

- Artichokes – 4, rinsed and trimmed
- Juice from 2 small lemons, freshly squeezed

Directions:

Add the ingredients in the Instant Pot and mix well. Close and cook on High for 10 minutes. Do a quick release when done. Serve.

Casserole
Cook time: 20 minutes| Serves: 8| Per serving: Calories 195; Carbs 1g; Fat 14g; Protein 11g

Ingredients:

- Eggs – 6
- Heavy cream – ½ cup
- Salt and freshly ground black pepper to taste
- Shredded cheddar cheese – 1 cup
- Fresh kale – 2 ½ cups, trimmed and chopped
- Small yellow onion – 1 chopped
- Herbs de Provence – 1 tsp.
- Water – 1 cup for the pot

Directions:

Add heavy cream, eggs, salt, and black pepper in a bowl and beat until mixed. Add remaining ingredients and mix well. Place the mixture into a baking dish evenly. Arrange a steamer trivet in the bottom of the Instant Pot and pour 1-cup water. Place the dish on top of the trivet. Cover and cook on High for 20 minutes. Serve.

Cheesy Broccoli
Cook time: 10 minutes| Serves: 2 | Per serving: Calories 536; Carbs 5g; Fat 47g; Protein 19g

Ingredients for the broccoli:

- Broccoli florets – 2 cups
- Olive oil – 1 tbsp.
- Garlic powder – 2 tsps.
- Smoked paprika – ½ tbsp.
- Salt and freshly ground black pepper
- Water – 1 cup for the pot

For Cheese Sauce

- Butter – 3 tbsps.
- Almond flour – 2 tbsps.
- Unsweetened almond milk – ½ cups
- Shredded cheddar cheese – 1 cup
- Garlic powder – 1 tsp.
- Salt to taste

Directions:

For the broccoli: in a bowl, add all the ingredients and toss to coat well. Arrange a steamer basket in the bottom of the Instant Pot and pour 1 cup of water. Place the broccoli on top of the steamer basket. Cover and cook on Low for 10 minutes. Meanwhile, for cheese sauce: in a pan melt butter over medium heat. Add flour and beat well. Slowly add almond milk and beat continuously. Cook until thickened, about 2 to 3 minutes. Stirring continuously. Add garlic powder, cheese, and salt and stir until smooth. Top the broccoli with the cheese sauce and serve.

Zesty Brussels Sprouts
Cook time: 4 minutes |Serves: 4| Per serving: Calories 157; Carbs 9g; Fat 3g; Protein 7.9g

Ingredients:

- Brussels sprouts – 2 pounds, trimmed
- Fresh lemon juice – ¼ cup
- Maple syrup – 2 tbsps.
- Butter – 1 tbsp.
- Lemon zest – 1 tsp. grated
- Black pepper to taste
- Salt to taste

Directions:

Stir the Brussels sprouts with maple syrup, lemon zest, lemon juice, butter, a pinch of salt and pepper into the Instant Pot. Cover and cook 4 minutes on High. Serve.

Steamed Artichokes
Cook time:10 minutes Serves: 4| Per serving: Calories 60; Carbs 6.6g; Fat 0.2g; Protein 4.2g

Ingredients:

- Medium artichokes – 4
- Lemon wedge – 1
- Water – 1 cup

Directions:

Wash the artichokes and cut off the stem. Rub the cut on top with the lemon, to prevent browning. Gently spread the leaves a bit. Place the artichokes in a steamer insert in the Instant Pot and pour in a cup of water. Cook for 10 minutes on High. Serve.

Cheesy Spinach
Cook time: 10 minutes| Serves: 3 | Per serving: Calories 169; Carbs 4.7g; Fat 8.7g; Protein 16.8g

Ingredients:

- Spinach – 2 lbs. chopped
- Eggs – 3

- Vegetable stock – 1 cup
- Parmesan cheese – ¼ cup, grated
- Chili pepper – 1 small, finely chopped
- Onion powder – 1 tsp.
- Garlic powder – ¼ tsp.
- Chili powder – ¼ tsp.
- Salt – 1 tsp.
- Cayenne pepper – ¼ tsp.
- Water - 1 cup

Directions:

Place the spinach in the Instant Pot. Add the vegetable broth and 1 cup of water. Sprinkle with salt and close the lid. Cook on High for 5 minutes. Open and press Sauté and add chili pepper. Sprinkle with cayenne pepper, salt, chili powder, onion powder, and garlic powder. Give it a good stir and cook until the liquid is reduced by half, about 5 minutes. Poach the eggs on top of the spinach and sprinkle all with Parmesan cheese. Serve.

Spinach Celery Stew
Cook time: 10 minutes| Serves: 4| Per serving: Calories 278; Carbs 4.3g; Fat 28.2g; Protein 2.3g

Ingredients:

- Fresh spinach – 2 cups, chopped
- Celery leaves – 1 cup, chopped
- Celery stalks – 1 cup, chopped
- Garlic – 2 cloves, minced
- Small onion – 1, chopped
- Heavy cream – 2 cups
- Lemon juice – 1 tbsp.
- Butter – 2 tbsps.
- Fresh mint – 1 tbsp. torn
- Salt – 1 tsp.
- Black pepper – ½ tsp. ground

Directions:

Press Sauté, add butter and constantly stir until melts. Add onions, garlic, and celery stalks. Cook for 2 minutes and add spinach and celery leaves. Sprinkle with salt and pepper. Cook for 2 to 3 minutes and pour in heavy cream. Cover and cook 5 minutes on High. Open and stir in the mint and lemon juice. Chill for 5 minutes and serve.

Cabbage Stew

Cook time: 25 minutes| Serves: 4| Per serving: Calories 338; Carbs 5.7g; Fat 28.8g; Protein 13.3g

Ingredients:

- Purple cabbage – 2 cups, shredded
- Bacon slices – 5, chopped
- Medium celery stalks – 2, chopped
- Medium red bell pepper – 1, chopped
- Vegetable stock – 2 cups
- Heavy cream – 1 cup
- Feta cheese – ½ cup, cubed
- Olive oil – 1 tbsp.
- Balsamic vinegar – 1 tsp.
- Sea salt – 1 tsp.
- Cayenne pepper – ½ tsp. ground
- Diced thyme – ½ tsp. ground
- Garlic powder – ½ tsp.

Directions:

Press sauté, add bacon and cook until crisp. Add red bell pepper, celery, and cabbage. Sprinkle with garlic powder, thyme, cayenne pepper, and salt. Pour in the vegetable stock and heavy cream. Cover and cook 15 minutes on High. Open the pot and stir in the feta cheese, vinegar, and olive oil. Press Sauté and cook for 5 minutes more. Serve.

Lemon Potatoes

Cook time: 8 minutes| Serves: 2| Per serving: Calories 185; Carbs 34g ; Fat 3.9g ; Protein 4.2g

Ingredients:

- White potatoes – 4
- Lemon zest – 1 tsp.
- Pink salt – 1 tsp.
- Fresh dill – 1 tbsp. chopped
- Dried oregano – 1 tsp.
- Lemon juice – 2 tbsps.
- Vegetable broth – ¼ cup
- Olive oil – 1 tbsp.

Directions:

Chop the potatoes. Whisk together lemon juice, olive oil, dried oregano, and fresh dill. Pour olive oil mixture over the potatoes and sprinkle with salt. Shake well and transfer in the Instant Pot. Add vegetable broth and cook on High for 8 minutes. Serve.

Mashed Potato

Cook time: 10 minutes |Serves: 6| Per serving: Calories 171; Carbs 34.2g; Fat 2.6g; Protein 3.9g

Ingredients:

- Potatoes – 6, peeled, chopped
- Water – 1 cup
- Coconut milk – ¼ cup
- Coconut yogurt – 1 tbsp.
- Salt – 1 tsp.
- Chives - 1 tbsp. chopped

Directions:

Place potato and water in the Instant Pot. Add salt and close the lid. Cook on High for 10 minutes. Open the lid, drain water from the potatoes and mash them. Add yogurt, coconut milk, and chopped chives. Mix until smooth and serve.

Sweet Potato Mash

Cook time: 9 minutes| Serves: 6| Per serving: Calories 67; Carbs 14.4g; Fat 0.3g; Protein 1.6g

Ingredients:

- Sweet potatoes – 2 cups, peeled, and chopped
- Salt – 1 tsp.
- Ground black pepper – 1 tsp.
- Vegetable broth – 1 cup
- Fresh parsley – 1 tbsp. chopped

Directions:

Put the potatoes, salt, and vegetable broth in the Instant Pot. Close the lid and cook on High for 9 minutes. Do a quick release and strain the sweet potatoes. Mash until smooth. Add chopped parsley and ground black pepper. Mix and serve.

Butter Corn

Cook time: 2 minutes | Serves: 4 | Per serving: Calories 229; Carbs 34.7g; Fat 9g; Protein 8.1g

Ingredients:

- Corn on the cob – 4
- Butter – 4 tsps.
- Salt – 1 tsp.
- Minced garlic – ½ tsp.
- Water – ½ cup

Directions:

Pour water in the Instant Pot and insert trivet. Place corn on the cobs on the trivet and close the lid. Cook on High for 2 minutes. Do a natural release. Churn together butter, salt, and minced garlic. Spread the corn on the cobs with the churned mixture and serve.

Tender Sweet Peppers

Cook time: 13 minutes| Serves: 4| Per serving: Calories 110; Carbs 11.5g; Fat 7.3g; Protein 2g

Ingredients:

- Red sweet peppers – 2
- Green bell pepper – 1
- Yellow sweet pepper – 1
- Garlic clove – 1, peeled
- Tomato – 1, chopped
- Fresh dill – ¼ cup, chopped
- Sesame oil - 2 tbsps.
- Water – ½ cup

Directions:

Cut the peppers into strips. Preheat the Instant Pot on Sauté. Add olive oil, garlic clove, and chopped tomato. Sauté the ingredients for 3 minutes. Mix. Add pepper strips and water. Close and cook on Sauté for 10 minutes. Serve.

Chapter 4 Rice, Grains, Beans

Polenta
Cook time: 8 minutes| Serves: 5| Per serving: Calories 156; Carbs 25.5g; Fat 2.8g; Protein 6.3g

Ingredients:

- Polenta – 1 cup
- Vegetable broth – 4 cups
- Coconut milk – 2 tbsps.
- Ground black pepper – ½ tsp.
- Salt – 1 tsp.

Directions:

Whisk together polenta and vegetable broth. Pour mixture in the Instant Pot. Add salt. Close and cook on High for 8 minutes. Do a quick release. Transfer cooked polenta in a bowl and stir well. Add ground black pepper and coconut milk. Stir and serve.

Proso Millet
Cook time: 15 minutes| Serves: 2| Per serving: Calories 436; Carbs 73.8g; Fat 7.9g; Protein 15.9g

Ingredients:

- Proso millet – 1 cup
- Vegetable broth – 2 cups
- Salt – 1 tsp.
- Chili flakes – ¼ tsp.
- Coconut oil – 1 tsp.

Directions:

Press Sauté and add the oil in the Instant Pot. Add salt, chili flakes, and proso millet. Stir it gently and cook for 3 minutes. Then add vegetable broth, and close. Cook on High for 10 minutes. Do a quick release. Open and serve.

Basmati Ragu
Cook time: 6 minutes| Serves: 4| Per serving: Calories 192; Carbs 42.4g; Fat 0.5g; Protein 4g

Ingredients:

- Basmati rice - 1 cup
- Water – 2 cups
- Sweet pepper – 1, chopped
- Red onion – 1, diced
- Salt – 1 tsp.

- Tomato paste – 1 tsp.
- Turmeric – 1 tsp.

Directions:

Mix together tomato paste, turmeric, salt, and water. Mix well. Pour it in the Instant Pot and add basmati rice. Close and cook on High for 3 minutes. Do a quick release and open the lid. Add sweet pepper and onion and mix well. Close and cook on High for 3 minutes more. Do a quick release. Open, stir, and serve.

Oatmeal with Onions

Cook time: 5 minutes| Serves: 5| Per serving: Calories 99; Carbs 13.4 g ; Fat 4.2g ; Protein 2.6g

Ingredients:

- Steel-cut oats – 2 cups
- Red onion – 1, sliced
- Coconut oil – 1 tbsp.
- Salt – ½ tsp.
- Water – 2 cups
- White pepper – ½ tsp.

Directions:

Preheat the Instant Pot on Sauté and add oil. Melt it and add onions, salt, and white pepper. Stir-fry for 2 minutes. Then add oats and water. Close the lid and cook on High for 3 minutes. Then do a natural release. Open, mix, and serve.

Teff in Tomato Paste

Cook time: 6 minutes| Serves: 3| Per serving: Calories 255; Carbs 45g ; Fat 3.2g ; Protein 11.3g

Ingredients:

- Teff - 1 cup
- Vegetable broth – 2 cups
- Salt – 1 tsp.
- Tomato paste – 1 tsp.
- Coconut oil – 1 tsp.

Directions:

Press Sauté and add oil. Add tomato paste and salt. Stir. Add teff and stir well. Sauté for 3 minutes. Add vegetable broth and close. Cook on High for 3 minutes. Then do a quick release. Open, mix, and serve.

Bean and Rice Casserole

Cook time: 30 minutes| Serves: 4| Per serving: Calories 192; Carbs 37.6g; Fat 1g; Protein 8.7g

Ingredients:

- Red beans – ¼ cup, soaked
- Black beans – 1/3 cup, soaked
- Brown rice – 1/3 cup
- Salt – 1 tsp.
- Barley – ¼ cup
- Water – 4 cups

Directions:

Place black and red beans in the Instant Pot. Add rice, salt, barley, and water. Close the lid and cook on Chili mode for 30 minutes. Do a natural release, open, and serve.

Rosemary Creamed Polenta

Cook time: 15 minutes| Serves: 5| Per serving: Calories 357; Carbs 51.7 g; Fat 14.8g; Protein 5.8g

Ingredients:

- Polenta – 2 cups
- Coconut cream – 1 cup
- Water – 3 cups
- Dried rosemary – 1 tsp.
- Pink salt – 1 tsp.
- Minced garlic - 1 tsp.
- Coconut oil - 1 tbsp.

Directions:

Place coconut oil in the Instant Pot and melt on Sauté. Add pink salt, minced garlic, and dried rosemary. Sauté for 3 minutes. Then add the coconut cream and bring the mixture to boil. Then add water and polenta. Mix. Close and cook on High for 8 minutes. Open and serve.

Shrimp Risotto

Cook time: 14 minutes| Serves: 4 | Per serving: Calories 476; Carbs 59g; Fat 12g; Protein 32g

Ingredients:

- Shrimp – 1 pound, peeled and deveined
- Brown rice – 1 ½ cups
- Olive oil – 3 tbsps.
- Fish stock – 3 cups
- Garlic – 2 tsps. minced
- Shallots – 2, chopped

- White wine – 4 tbsps.
- Salt and pepper, to taste

Directions:

Heat oil on Sauté in the Instant Pot. Add garlic and onion. Cook for 3 minutes. Add shrimp and cook for 3 minutes or until lightly browned. Stir in the remaining ingredients and cover. Cook on 8 minutes on Rice at High. Do a quick release, open, and serve.

Spinach Vermouth Risotto
Cook time: 13 minutes| Serves: 4| Per serving: Calories 327; Carbs 44g; Fat 8g; Protein 10g

Ingredients:

- Mushrooms – 1 cup, sliced
- Spinach – 2 cups, chopped
- Vermouth – ½ cup
- Rice – 1 cup
- Zucchini – 1, sliced
- Parmesan cheese – ½ cup, shredded
- Shallot - 1, chopped
- Garlic – 1 tsp. minced
- Olive oil – 1 tbsp.
- Chicken stock – 2 cups

Directions:

Heat oil on Sauté in the Instant Pot. Cook the shallot and garlic for two minutes. Add mushrooms and cook for 3 minutes more. Stir in the rest of the ingredients, except the cheese. Cover and cook on 8 minutes on Rice at High. Do a quick release. Open and stir in the cheese. Serve.

Tomato Risotto
Cook time: 10 minutes |Serves: 4| Per serving: Calories 348; Carbs 61.4g; Fat 7.1g; Protein 8.5g

Ingredients:

- Olive oil – 2 tbsps.
- Onion – 1, chopped
- Rice – 1 ½ cups
- Vegetable broth – 2 cups
- Tomato sauce – ¾ cup
- Cumin – 1 tsp.
- Garlic powder – 1 tsp.
- Salt – ¼ tsp.

Directions:

Heat the oil on Sauté in the Instant Pot. Add onion and salt and cook for 3 minutes. Add broth and tomato sauce and simmer for 2 minutes. Add rice and season with salt, pepper, garlic powder, and cumin. Cover and cook on Rice mode for 6 minutes. Do a quick release, open, and serve.

Baked Beans
Cook time: 55 minutes| Serves: 4| Per serving: Calories 238; Carbs 46g; Fat 1g; Protein 13g

Ingredients:

- White beans - 1 cup
- Water – 5 cups
- Tomato paste – 2 tbsps.
- Salt – 1 tsp.
- Dried dill - 1 tsp.
- Brown sugar – 1 tsp.
- Barbecue sauce - ½ cup
- Vegetable broth – ½ cup
- Carrot – 1, chopped
- Ground black pepper – ½ tsp.

Directions:

Place the white beans and water into the Instant Pot. Close and cook on High for 30 minutes. Do a quick release, open and drain water from beans. Add tomato paste, salt, dried dill, barbecue sauce, broth, chopped carrot, and ground black pepper. Mix and close the lid. Press Sauté and cook for 25 minutes more. Open and serve.

Black Beans
Cook time: 45 minutes| Serves: 4| Per serving: Calories 278; Carbs 45.5g; Fat 4.4g; Protein 15.8g

Ingredients:

- Black beans – 1 ½ cups
- Water – 3 cups
- Salt – 1 tsp.
- Peppercorn – ¼ tsp.
- Chives – 1 tbsp. chopped
- Coconut oil – 1 tbsp.
- Chili flakes – 1 tsp.

Directions:

Add water, black beans, salt, and peppercorn into the Instant Pot. Close and cook on High for 30 minutes. Open and add chili flakes, chives, coconut oil, and mix well. Close and press Sauté. Sauté for 15 minutes. Serve.

Red Kidney Beans Burrito

Cook time:15 minutes| Serves: 2| Per serving: Calories 352; Carbs 40.3g; Fat 17.6g; Protein 12.4g

Ingredients:

- Avocado – ½, sliced
- Bell pepper – 1, sliced
- Onion – ½, chopped
- Olive oil - 1 tbsp.
- Tomato paste – 1 tsp.
- Chili flakes – ½ tsp.
- Red kidney beans – ½ cup, canned
- Ground cumin – ½ tsp.
- Ground coriander - ½ tsp.
- Fresh cilantro – ½ cup, chopped
- Flour tortillas – 2

Directions:

Preheat the Instant Pot on Sauté for 3 minutes. Pour olive oil and add sliced bell pepper. Stir-fry for 2 to 3 minutes. Add chopped onion, chili flakes, ground cumin, coriander, and tomato paste. Stir and add red kidney beans. Mix it up. Close and Sauté for 10 minutes. Open and fill the tortillas with the bean mixture, add cilantro, avocado, and roll. Serve.

Cowboy Caviar

Cook time: 6 minutes| Serves: 4| Per serving: Calories 99; Carbs 7.6g; Fat 7.5g; Protein 2.1g

Ingredients:

- Black-eyed peas – ½ cup
- Water – 1 cup
- Tomatoes – 4, chopped
- Apple cider vinegar – 1 tbsp.
- Lemon juice – 1 tbsp.
- Jalapeno pepper – 1, chopped
- Fresh parsley - ½ cup, chopped
- Olive oil – 2 tbsps.
- Salt – ½ tsp.

Directions:

Add the water and peas in the Instant Pot and close. Cook on High for 6 minutes. Then do a quick release. In a bowl, mix tomatoes, jalapeno pepper, parsley, and apple cider vinegar. Add chilled black-eyed peas to the mixture. Add olive oil, salt, and lemon juice. Mix and serve.

Creamy Kidney Beans

Cook time: 25 minutes| Serves: 4| Per serving: Calories 620; Carbs 64 g; Fat 33g; Protein 23.7g

Ingredients:

- Kidney beans – 2 cups
- Water – 2 cups
- Almond milk – 2 cups
- Coconut oil – 1 tbsp.
- Salt – 1 tsp.
- Tomato paste – 1 tbsp.
- Garlic – 1 clove, peeled
- Taco seasoning – 1 tbsp.

Directions:

Place water, kidney beans, almond milk, coconut oil, salt, tomato paste, garlic clove, and taco seasoning in the Instant Pot. Mix and close. Cook on High for 25 minutes. Then do a quick release. Mix and serve.

Green Bean and Lentil Stew

Cook time: 20 minutes| Serves: 5| Per serving: Calories 410; Carbs 64.4g ; Fat 7.7g ; Protein 28.8g

Ingredients:

- Olive oil – 2 tbsps.
- Celery stalks – ½ cup, chopped
- Parsnips – ½ cup, chopped
- Green bell pepper – 1, chopped
- Red bell pepper – 1, chopped
- Poblano pepper – 1, chopped
- Leeks – ½ cup, chopped
- Ginger-garlic paste – 1 tsp.
- Dried basil – ½ tsp.
- Dried oregano – ½ tsp.
- Dried rosemary – ½ tsp.
- Curry paste – ½ tsp.
- Brown lentils – 2 cups
- Vegetable broth – 3 cups
- Tomato paste – ½ cup
- Salt and pepper to taste
- Green beans – 2 cups, trimmed and halved

Directions:

Heat the oil in the Instant Pot on Sauté. Add the celery, parsnip, peppers, and leeks and stir-fry for 5 minutes. Stir in aromatics, curry paste, lentils, broth, and tomato paste. Season with salt and pepper. Cover the pot. Cook on High for 10 minutes. Open and the green beans and press Sauté. Sauté for 5 minutes. Serve.

Biryani Rice

Cook time: 27 minutes| Serves: 2| Per serving: Calories 420; Carbs 92g; Fat 3g; Protein 8.3g

Ingredients:

- Red onion – ¼ cup, diced
- Garlic clove – 1, minced
- Turmeric powder – ½ tsp.
- Cumin seeds – 1 tsp.
- Cinnamon stick – 1
- Salt – ¼ tsp.
- Brown rice – 1 cup, soaked 10 minutes, then drained
- Water – 1 ½ cups
- Raisins – ¼ cup
- Mint – ¼ cup, chopped
- Raw cashew, chopped
- Fresh mint leaves
- Fresh cilantro

Directions:

Press Sauté on your Instant Pot. Add cumin seeds, diced red onion, minced garlic, turmeric powder, cinnamon, and salt to the Instant Pot. Stir-fry for 1 minute. Add brown rice and stir. Cover and cook on Multigrain for 25 minutes. Do a quick release and open. Add raisins and chopped mint. Mix. Serve the rice garnished with fresh mint leaves and chopped cashews.

Potato and Green Bean Salad

Cook time: 7 minutes| Serves: 6| Per serving: Calories 218; Carbs 40.4g; Fat 5.1g; Protein 6.3g

Ingredients:

- Large potatoes – 3, skinned and chopped
- Frozen green beans – 2 large bags (about 2 pounds)
- Mushrooms – 1 cup
- Water – 1 ½ cup
- Olive oil – 2 tbsps.
- Dash of sea salt
- Splash of lemon juice
- Pepper to taste

Directions:

Add lemon juice, water, salt, pepper, mushrooms, and potatoes to the Instant Pot. Place a steamer basket. Place green beans on top of the steamer basket and drizzle with oil. Cover and cook on High 7 minutes. Open and pour the beans into a strainer, then place on a large bowl. Mix the green beans and the rest of the ingredients from the Instant Pot. Serve.

Green Chili Baked Beans

Cook time: 30 minutes| Serves: 4| Per serving: Calories 435; Carbs 89g; Fat 4g; Protein 21g

Ingredients:

- Blackstrap molasses – ¼ cup
- Maple syrup – ¼ cup
- Packed light brown sugar – ¼ cup
- Ketchup – 2 tbsps.
- Worcestershire sauce – 1 tbsp.
- Olive oil – 1 tbsp.
- Sweet onion – 1 small, chopped
- Garlic – 3 to 4, minced
- Salt – 1 tsp.
- Dried navy beans – 1 pound, soaked in water overnight, rinsed and drained
- Diced roasted green chilies – 1 ½ cups
- Apple cider vinegar – 1 tsp.

Directions:

In a bowl, whisk the sauce, ketchup, brown sugar, maple syrup, and molasses. Press Sauté on the Instant Pot and add oil. Add onion and garlic. Stir-fry for 2 minutes. Add molasses mix, beans, and salt and mix. Cover the Instant Pot. Cook on High for 30 minutes. Open the lid and press Sauté. Stir in green chilies and simmer until thickens about 5 to 10 minutes. Serve.

Refried Pinto Beans

Cook time: 32 minutes| Serves: 6| Per serving: Calories 310; Carbs 53g; Fat 6g; Protein 17g

Ingredients:

- Olive oil - 1 tbsp.
- Onion – 1, quartered
- Garlic – 3 cloves, peeled
- Dried pinto beans – 1 pound, rinsed
- Vegetable stock – 2 quarts
- Ground cumin – 1 tsp.
- Dried Mexican oregano – 1 tsp.
- Chili powder – ½ tsp.
- Ground black pepper – ¼ tsp.
- Lime juice – 1 tbsp.

- Salt to taste

Directions:

In the Instant Pot, combine pepper, chili powder, oregano, cumin, stock, beans, garlic, onion, and oil. Cover and cook on High for 32 minutes. Do a natural release and open. Remove most of the remaining liquid. Blend with a hand mixer until smooth. Add cooking water as needed. Stir in salt and lime juice. Serve.

Chickpea Basil Salad
Cook time: 38 minutes| Serves: 2 | Per serving: Calories 396; Carbs 67g; Fat 6g; Protein 21g

Ingredients:

- Dried chickpeas – 1 cup, rinsed
- Enough water to cover chickpeas by 3 to 4 inches
- Fresh basil leaves – 1 cup, chopped
- Grape tomatoes – 1 ½ cups, halved
- Balsamic vinegar – 2 tbsps.
- Garlic powder – ½ tsp.
- Salt – to taste

Directions:

Combine the water and chickpeas in the Instant Pot. Cover and cook on High for 38 minutes. Do a natural release and open. Drain the chickpeas. Cool. Stir together the salt, garlic powder, vinegar, tomatoes, and basil in a bowl. Add the beans and mix. Serve.

Cilantro Lime Brown Rice
Cook time: 19 minutes| Serves: 4| Per serving: Calories 344; Carbs 72g; Fat 3g; Protein 7g

Ingredients:

- Brown rice – 2 cups, rinsed and drained
- Water – 2 ½ cups
- Fresh cilantro – 1/3 cup, chopped
- Juice of 1 lime
- Zest of 1 lime
- Dash ground cumin
- Salt to taste

Directions:

In the Instant Pot, combine the water and rice. Cover and cook on High for 19 minutes. Open and stir in cumin, lime juice, zest, and cilantro. Season with salt. Serve.

Chapter 5 Soups and Stews

Lamb Stew
Cook time: 1 hour 25 minutes | Serves: 8 | Per serving: Calories 462; Carbs 1.2g; Fat 37g; Protein 30g

Ingredients:

- Lamb tallow – ½ cup
- Garlic – 3 cloves, crushed
- Onion – 1 large, diced
- Rosemary – ¼ cup, chopped
- Celery – 3 sticks, diced
- Salt – 1 tsp.
- Ground black pepper – 1 tsp.
- Red wine vinegar – ½ cup
- Tomato puree – 1 cup
- Beef broth – 4 cups
- Lamb shoulder – 4 lbs. (cut into 1 ½ inch chunks)
- Mushrooms – ½ lbs. (cut into ½ inch slices)
- Sour cream – 1 cup
- Parmesan cheese – ½ cup
- Water as needed

Directions:

Place the tallow, celery, rosemary, onions, and garlic in the instant pot. Press Sauté and cook for 5 minutes. Stirring occasionally. Add the tomato puree, vinegar, salt and pepper and cook for 5 more minutes. Add the beef broth, mix and then add the lamb chunks. Add water until the lamb is just covered. Cover and cook on Meat/Stew for 60 minutes. When done, do a natural release. Press Sauté and add sliced mushrooms. Cook for 15 minutes. Serve hot, topped with 1 tbsp. grated parmesan cheese and 2 tbsps. of sour cream.

Rabbit Cabbage Stew
Cook time: 35 minutes | Serves: 4 | Per serving: Calories 543; Carbs 1.8g; Fat 24.3g; Protein 74g

Ingredients:

- Whole rabbit – 1, cleaned
- Cabbage – 1 cup, shredded
- Beef broth – 4 cups
- Butter – 3 tbsps.
- Salt – 1 tsp.
- Freshly ground white pepper – ½ tsp.
- Cayenne pepper – 1 tsp.

Directions:

Combine all the ingredients in instant pot and season with spices. Stir to mix well. Cover and cook 35 minutes on High. Serve warm.

Pork Meatball Stew

Cook time: 30 minutes | Serves: 10 | Per serving: Calories 530; Carbs 11g; Fat 29g; Protein 42g

Ingredients:

- Minced pork – 3 lbs.
- Almond meal – 2 cups
- Vegetable broth – 1 cup
- Tomato passata – 1 cup
- Celeriac – 1, cubed
- Onion – 1, chopped
- Collards – 2 lbs. chopped
- Eggs – 4
- Olive oil– 1 tbsp.

Directions:

In a bowl, mix the eggs, almonds, and meat. Make the meat into balls. Add oil in the instant pot and brown the meatballs for 5 minutes. Add broth and sauce. Cover and cook on Stew for 5 minutes. Open and add the vegetables. Seal and cook on Stew for 20 minutes more. Serve.

Worcestershire Chili

Cook time: 38 minutes | Serves: 4 | Per serving: Calories 304; Carbs 9.3g; Fat 10g; Protein 37g

Ingredients:

- Ground beef – 1 pound
- Carrot – 1, diced
- Canned diced tomatoes – 26 ounces
- Chili powder – 1 tbsp.
- Garlic powder – 1 tsp.
- Onion powder – 1 tsp.
- Paprika – 1 tsp.
- Onion – 1, diced
- Parsley – 1 tbsp.
- Salt – 1 tsp.
- Worcestershire chili – 1 tbsp.
- Oil – 1 tbsp.
- Cauliflower rice – 1 cup

Directions:

Heat the oil in the instant pot on Sauté setting. Add the beef and cook for 5 minutes. Add onion and all to the spices and cook for 3 minutes. Except for the cauliflower, stir in the remaining ingredients. Cook for 20 minutes on Meat/Stew. Add cauliflower rice and cook for 10 minutes. Release the pressure naturally. Serve.

Spiced Chili

Cook time: 40 minutes| Serves: 10 | Per serving: Calories 305; Carbs 1g; Fat 10.7g; Protein 43.7g

Ingredients:

- Olive oil – 1 tbsp.
- Ground beef – 3 pounds
- Chopped yellow onion – ½
- Ground cumin – 2 tbsps.
- Smoked paprika – 1 tbsp.
- Ground chipotle – 1 tbsp.
- Salt and freshly ground black pepper to taste
- Sugar-free tomato paste – 1 (6-ounce)
- Green chiles – 1 (4-ounce) can
- Homemade beef broth – 2 cups
- Soy sauce – 2 tbsps.
- Fresh lemon juice – 1 tbsp.
- Xanthan gum – ½ tsp.

Directions:

Add oil in the instant pot and press Sauté. Then add onion and beef and cook for 9 minutes. Add the spices and cook for 1 minute. Stir in tomato paste, green chiles, and broth. Cook on High for 25 minutes. Open and press Sauté. Stir in the lemon juice and soy sauce. Slowly add the xanthan gum. Stir continuously. Serve.

Italian Sausage and Kale Soup

Cook time: 5 minutes| Serves: 6 | Per serving: Calories 400; Carbs 7g; Fat 33g; Protein 16g

Ingredients:

- Hot Italian sausage stuffing – 1 lbs.
- Onion – 1 cup, diced
- Garlic – 6 cloves, minced
- Cauliflower – 12 oz. frozen
- Kale – 12 oz. frozen
- Water – 3 cups
- Heavy cream – ½ cup
- Parmesan cheese – ½ cup, grated

Directions:

Press Sauté add the sausage and lightly brown for 2 minutes. Constantly stir and break into smaller pieces. Add the garlic and onions and mix thoroughly to combine. Add the kale, cauliflower and three cups of water. Cover and cook 3 minutes on High. Open and slowly stir in the cream. Serve sprinkled with parmesan. Serve.

Broccoli and Cauliflower Soup

Cook time: 25 minutes| Serves: 4 | Per serving: Calories 172; Carbs 10.9g; Fat 8.9g; Protein 10.7g

Ingredients:

- Broccoli – 1 lb. chopped
- Cauliflower – 2 cups, chopped into florets
- Vegetables broth – 3 cups
- Milk – 1 cup
- Sour cream – ½ cup
- Salt – ½ tsp.
- Dried rosemary – ½ tsp.

Directions:

Add broccoli, cauliflower, and broth into the Instant Pot and cover. Cook for 20 minutes on High. Open and chill for a while, then transfer to a food processor and process until smooth. Pour the soup back into the pot and press Sauté. Bring the mixture to a boil and add milk. Sprinkle with salt and dried rosemary. Stir well and cook for 2 to 3 minutes. Stir in the sour cream and cook for 1 minute. Serve.

Italian Chicken Soup

Cook time: 10 minutes| Serves: 6| Per serving: Calories 183; Carbs 3.3g; Fat 6.9g; Protein 25.3g

Ingredients:

- Bone broth – 4 cups
- Chicken – 1 pound, ground
- Hot peppers – ½ tsp. chopped
- Dried basil – ½ tsp.
- Rosemary – ½ tsp. ground
- Dried oregano – ½ tsp.
- Salt – ½ tsp.
- Ground black pepper – ½ tsp.
- Coconut oil – 2 tbsps.
- Fire roasted tomatoes – 1 (14-ounce) can

Directions:

Add everything in the Instant Pot. Close and cook on High for 10 minutes. Open and serve.

Butternut Squash Soup

Cook time: 10 minutes| Serves: 6| Per serving: Calories 278; Carbs 9g; Fat 23.7g; Protein 7.4g

Ingredients:

- Coconut oil – 2 tbsps.
- Garlic – 4 cloves, minced
- Bone broth – 6 cups

- Butternut squash – 2 cups, cubed
- Curry powder – ½ tsp.
- Ginger – ½ tsp. grated
- Salt – ½ tsp.
- Ground black pepper – ½ tsp.
- Full-fat coconut milk – 2 cups

Directions:

Press Sauté and add oil. Add the garlic and sauté for 2 minutes. Add squash, salt, pepper, ginger, curry powder, and bone broth to the Instant Pot. Close and cook 10 minutes on High. Open and pour in the coconut milk and blend with a hand mixer. Serve.

Hearty Hamburger Soup

Cook time: 25 minutes |Serves: 4| Per serving: Calories 514; Carbs 9g; Fat 30.2g; Protein 49.4g

Ingredients:

- Coconut oil – 2 tbsps.
- Ground beef – 1 pound
- Bone broth – 4 cups
- Bacon – 3 slices, cooked and chopped
- Full-fat cheddar cheese – 1 cup, shredded
- Carrot – 1, chopped
- Celery – 1 stalk, chopped
- Dried parsley - ½ tsp.
- Crushed red pepper – ½ tsp.
- Dried basil – ½ tsp.
- Salt – ½ tsp.
- Freshly ground black pepper – ½ tsp.
- Diced tomatoes – 1 (14-ounce) can

Directions:

Add the oil in the Instant Pot and melt on Sauté. Add the beef and brown for 2 to 5 minutes. Add tomatoes, black pepper, salt, basil, red pepper, parsley, celery, carrot, cheese, bacon, and broth. Close and cook on High for 25 minutes. Do a natural release and serve.

Pumpkin and Bacon Soup

Cook time: 10 minutes |Serves: 4| Per serving: Calories 578; Carbs 8.3g; Fat 51.2g; Protein 17.4g

Ingredients:

- Coconut oil – 2 tbsps.
- Bacon – 4 slices, cooked and chopped
- Bone broth – 2 cups

- Pumpkin puree – 2 cups
- Full-fat coconut milk – 2 cups
- Full-fat cheddar cheese – ½ cup, shredded
- Crushed red pepper – ½ tsp.
- Salt – ½ tsp.
- Freshly ground black pepper – ½ tsp.
- Heavy whipping cream – ¼ cup

Directions:

Add all the ingredients to the Instant Pot and mix well. Close and cook 10 minutes on Low. Serve.

Clam Chowder

Cook time: 8 minutes| Serves: 6| Per serving: Calories 314; Carbs 7.8g; Fat 26.7g; Protein 5.2g

Ingredients:

- Full-fat coconut milk – 2 cups
- Bay leaves – 2
- Bone broth – 1 cup
- Cauliflower – 1 pound, chopped
- Celery – 1 cup, chopped
- Ground black pepper – ½ tsp.
- Salt – ½ tsp.
- Small onion – ¼, thinly sliced
- Clams – 2 (7-ounce) cans, chopped and drained
- Heavy whipping cream – 1 cup

Directions:

Add the onion, salt, black pepper, celery, cauliflower, bone broth, bay leaves, and coconut milk to the Instant Pot. Mix well. Close and cook 5 minutes on high. Open and remove bay leaves and stir in the clams and whipping cream. Press Sauté and cook for 2 to 3 minutes. Serve.

Mexican Soup

Cook time: 17 minutes |Serves: 8| Per serving: Calories 395; Carbs 1.6g; Fat 20.5g; Protein 40g

Ingredients:

- Boneless, skinless chicken breasts – 2 pounds
- Salsa – 1 (15-ounce) jar
- Diced green chilies – 1 (4-ounce) can
- Ground cumin – 2 tbsps.
- Red chili powder – 1 tbsp.
- Garlic powder – 1 tsp.
- Salt and freshly ground black pepper to taste

- Chicken broth – 5 cups
- Water – 1 cup
- Softened and chopped cream cheese – 1 (8-ounce) block

Directions:

In the pot, add all ingredients except cream cheese. Mix to combine. Cook on High for 15 minutes. Remove the lid and transfer the chicken breasts into a bowl. Shred chicken breasts with two forks, and then return to the pot. Press Sauté and stir in cream cheese. Cook for 1 to 2 minutes, stirring continuously. Serve.

Cheesy Pepper Soup

Cook time: 22 minutes| Serves: 6| Per serving: Calories 504; Carbs 1g; Fat 23g; Protein 56g

Ingredients:

- Butter – 3 tbsps.
- Seeded and chopped green bell pepper - ½
- Yellow onion – ½, chopped
- Seeded and chopped jalapeno peppers – 2
- Garlic cloves – 2, minced
- Ground cumin – 1 tsp.
- Paprika – ¼ tsp.
- Salt and black pepper to taste
- Cubed boneless, skinless chicken breasts – 1 ½ pound
- Cream cheese – 6 ounces
- Chicken broth – 3 cups
- Heavy whipping cream – ½ cup
- Cheddar cheese – ¾ cup
- Monterrey Jack Cheese – ¾ cup
- Cooked and crumbled bacon - ½ pound
- Xanthan gum – ½ tsp.

Directions:

Press Sauté and add the bell pepper, onion, jalapenos, garlic, and spices and cook for 5 minutes. Stir in chicken, cream cheese and bacon. Cover and cook on High for 15 minutes. Then open and press Sauté. Add bacon, cheeses, and cream and stir until smooth. Sprinkle xanthan gum on top of soup and cook for 1 to 2 minutes. Serve hot.

Cheddar Chicken Soup

Cook time: 15 minutes| Serves: 4| Per serving: Calories 513; Carbs 4g; Fat 31g; Protein 39g

Ingredients:

- Chopped yellow onion – ¼ cup
- Garlic clove – 1, minced
- Hot sauce – ¼ cup
- Boneless, skinless chicken thighs – 2 (6-ounces, each)
- Chopped celery – ½ cup
- Butter – 2 tbsps.
- Chicken broth – 3 cups
- Shredded cheddar cheese – 2 cups
- Heavy cream – 1 cup

Directions:

Except for the cheese and cream, add the rest of the ingredients in the Instant Pot and mix. Close and cook on High for 15 minutes. Then open and remove the cooked meat and shred it. Add the shredded meat back in the potting mix. Mix in the cream and cheese. Stir to mix well. Enjoy.

Beef Cabbage Soup

Cook time: 20 minutes |Serves: 4| Per serving: Calories 246; Carbs 8g; Fat 17g; Protein 19g

Ingredients:

- Garlic – 1 clove, minced
- Finely ground beef – 1 pound
- Water – 2 cups
- Coconut oil – 1 tbsp.
- Onion - ½ diced
- Black pepper and salt to taste
- Cabbage – ½ head, chopped

Directions:

Press Sauté and add oil to the Instant Pot. Add the onion and garlic and stir-fry for 2 minutes. Add the meat and brown for 3 minutes. Pour in water and season to taste. Mix. Close and press Poultry. Cook 10 minutes on High. Open and mix in the cabbage. Press Sauté and cook 5 minutes. Serve.

Summer Vegetable Soup

Cook time: 6 minutes| Serves: 6| Per serving: Calories 210; Carbs 10g; Fat 14g; Protein 10g

Ingredients:

- Finely sliced leeks – 3 cups
- Chopped rainbow chard – 6 cups, stems and leaves

- Chopped celery – 1 cup
- Minced garlic – 2 tbsps. divided
- Dried oregano – 1 tsp.
- Salt – 1 tsp.
- Black pepper – 2 tsps.
- Chicken broth – 3 cups, plus more as needed
- Sliced yellow summer squash – 2 cups
- Chopped fresh parsley – ¼ cup
- Heavy whipping cream – ¾ cup
- Grated Parmesan cheese – 6 tbsps.

Directions:

Put the chard, leeks, celery, 1 tbsp. garlic, oregano, salt, pepper, and broth into the Instant Pot. Cover and cook on High for 3 minutes. Open and press Sauté. Add the remaining 1 tbsp. garlic, parsley, and squash. Cook for 3 minutes. Stir in the cream. Sprinkle with Parmesan and serve.

Creamy Tomato Basil Soup
Cook time: 4 minutes| Serves: 4 | Per serving: Calories 265; Carbs 20,9g ; Fat 12g ; Protein 9g

Ingredients:

- Butter – 2 tbsps.
- Small sweet onion – 1, chopped
- Garlic – 2 cloves, minced
- Carrot – 1, chopped
- Celery – 1 stalk, chopped
- Vegetable stock – 3 cups
- Tomatoes – 3 pounds, quartered
- Fresh basil – ¼ cup, plus more for garnishing
- Salt and ground black pepper
- Milk – 1 cup

Directions:

Press Sauté on the Instant Pot add butter and melt. Add the garlic and onion and stir-fry for 4 minutes. Add celery and carrot and cook 2 minutes more. Stir continuously. Add the stock and deglaze the pot. Add salt, basil, and tomatoes. Stir to mix. Cover and cook on High for 4 minutes. Open and blend with a hand mixer until smooth. Stir in milk. Taste and adjust seasoning. Garnish and serve.

Split Pea Soup
Cook time: 15 minutes| Serves: 4| Per serving: Calories 224; Carbs 35g; Fat 5g; Protein 13g

Ingredients:

- Roasted walnut oil – 1 tbsp.
- Carrots – 2, diced
- Celery – 1 stalk, diced
- Dried thyme – 1 tsp.
- Smoked paprika – 1 tsp.
- Bay leaf – 1
- Salt – ½ to 1 tsp. plus more as needed
- Garlic – 2 cloves, minced
- Green split peas – 1 cup
- Vegetable stock – 2 ½ cups
- Ground black pepper

Directions:

Press Sauté on the Instant Pot. Add oil. Add salt, bay leaf, paprika, thyme, celery, and carrots. Stir-fry for 3 minutes, then add garlic and cook for 30 seconds more. Stir in the split peas and stock. Cover and cook on High for 15 minutes. Open and discard the bay leaf. Taste and adjust seasoning and serve.

Sweet Potato Stew
Cook time: 10 minutes| Serves: 4| Per serving: Calories 224; Carbs 26g; Fat 13g; Protein 5g

Ingredients:

- Avocado oil – 2 tbsps.
- Sweet onion – ½, diced
- Sweet potatoes – 2, peeled and cubed
- Garlic – 2 cloves, minced
- Salt – 1 to 1 ½ tsp.
- Ground turmeric – 1 tsp.
- Paprika – 1 tsp.
- Ground cumin – ½ tsp.
- Dried oregano – ½ tsp.
- Chili powder – 1 to 2 dashes
- Roma tomatoes – 2, chopped
- Lite coconut milk – 1 (14-ounce) can, shaken well
- Water – 1 ¼ cups, plus more as needed
- Chopped kale – 1 to 2 cups

Directions:

Press Sauté on the Instant pot and add oil. Add onion and stir-fry for 3 minutes. Stir in chili powder, oregano, cumin, paprika, turmeric, salt, garlic, and sweet potatoes. Stir-fry for 1 minute. Add the water, tomatoes, and coconut milk and mix. Cover and cook on High for 4 minutes. Open and stir in the kale. Mix. Serve.

White Bean & Swiss Chard Stew

Cook time: 7 minutes| Serves: 4| Per serving: Calories 174; Carbs 29g; Fat4g; Protein 9g

Ingredients:

- Olive oil – 1 tbsp.
- Carrots – 2, chopped
- Celery – 1 stalk, sliced
- Onion – ½, chopped
- Garlic – 2 to 3 cloves, minced
- Tomatoes – 3, chopped
- Red pepper flakes – ¼ to ½ tsp.
- Dried rosemary – ½ tsp.
- Dried oregano – ½ tsp.
- Dried basil – ¼ tsp.
- Salt – ½ tsp. plus more as needed
- Ground black pepper to taste
- Cooked great northern beans – 2 cups
- Swiss chard leaves – 1 small bunch, chopped

Directions:

Press Sauté on the Instant Pot and add oil. Add onion, celery, and carrots and stir-fry for 3 minutes. Add garlic and cook for 30 seconds. Stir in beans, pepper, salt, basil, oregano, rosemary, red pepper flakes, and tomatoes. Cover and cook on High for 3 minutes. Open and stir in Swiss chard. Wilt for 3 minutes. Taste and adjust seasoning. Serve.

Butternut Quinoa Chili

Cook time: 7 minutes| Serves: 4| Per serving: Calories 325; Carbs 61g; Fat 7g; Protein 10g

Ingredients:

- Olive oil –2 tbsps.
- Carrots – 2, sliced
- Sweet onion – 1, chopped
- Red bell pepper – 1, chopped
- Jalapeno pepper – 1, diced
- Garlic cloves – 1, minced
- Butternut squash – 1, peeled and chopped
- Diced tomatoes with juice – 1 (14-ounce) can

- Uncooked quinoa – 1 cup, rinsed
- Vegetable stock – 2 ½ cups
- Bay leaf – 1
- Ground cumin – 1 tsp.
- Salt – ½ to 1 tsp. plus more if needed
- Sweet paprika – ½ tsp.
- Chili powder – ½ tsp. or more to taste
- Ground black pepper to taste
- Lemon juice – 1 tbsp.

Directions:

Press Sauté and add oil. Add jalapeno, bell pepper, onion, and carrots. Stir-fry for 3 minutes. Add garlic and cook for 30 seconds. Add the pepper, chili powder, paprika, salt, cumin, bay leaf, stock, quinoa, tomatoes, and squash. Cover and cook for 7 minutes on High. Open and discard the bay leaf. Stir in the lemon juice. Taste and adjust seasoning. Serve.

Curried Squash Soup

Cook time: 30 minutes| Serves: 4| Per serving: Calories 267; Carbs 50g; Fat 11g; Protein 5g

Ingredients:

- Olive oil - 1 tbsp.
- Onion – 1, chopped
- Garlic – 2 cloves, chopped
- Curry powder – 1 tbsp.
- Butternut squash – 1 (2 to 3-pound), cubed
- Vegetable stock – 4 cups
- Salt – 1 tsp.
- Lite coconut milk – 1 (14-ounce) can

Directions:

Press Sauté on the Instant Pot. Add oil. Add onion and stir-fry for 3 to 4 minutes. Add curry powder and garlic and cook for 1 minute. Add the stock, squash, and salt. Cover and cook on High for 25 minutes. Open the pot and blend with a hand mixer. Stir in the coconut milk and serve.

Chapter 6 Vegetable Recipes

Minestrone Soup

Cook time: 7 minutes |Serves: 4| Per serving: Calories 332; Carbs 54g; Fat 12g; Protein 13g

Ingredients:

- Olive oil – 2 tbsps.
- Celery stalks – 2, sliced
- Sweet onion – 1, diced
- Large carrot – 1, sliced
- Garlic – 2 cloves, minced
- Dried oregano – 1 tsp.
- Dried basil – 1 tsp.
- Salt – ½ tsp. to 1 tsp. plus more as needed
- Bay leaf – 1
- Zucchini – 1, diced
- Diced tomatoes – 1 (28-ounce) can
- Kidney beans – 1 (16-ounce) can, drained and rinsed
- Dried pasta – 1 cup
- Vegetable stock – 6 cups
- Fresh baby spinach – 2 to 3 cups
- Ground black pepper

Directions:

Press Sauté on your Instant Pot. Add oil, carrot, onion, and celery. Stir-fry for 2 to 3 minutes. Now add garlic and stir-fry for 1 minute. Add bay leaf, salt, basil, and oregano. Stir and let sit for 30 seconds. Add the stock, pasta, kidney beans, tomatoes, and zucchini. Cover the Instant Pot. Cook on High for 3 minutes. Open and discard the bay leaf. Stir in spinach. Taste and adjust seasoning. Serve.

Chipotle Sweet Potato Chowder

Cook time: 2 minutes| Serves: 4| Per serving: Calories 216; Carbs 35g; Fat 10g; Protein 5g

Ingredients:

- Vegetable stock – 1 ¼ cups
- Lite coconut milk – 1 (14-ounce) can
- Sweet potatoes – 2, peeled and diced
- Canned chipotle peppers – 2 to 4 (in adobo sauce), diced
- Red bell pepper – 1, diced
- Small onion – 1, diced
- Ground cumin – 1 tsp.

- Salt – ½ to 1 tsp.
- Frozen sweet corn – 1 ½ cups
- Adobo sauce from the canned peppers, to taste

Directions:

Whisk the coconut milk and stock in a bowl. Mix well. Pour into the Instant Pot. Add the salt, cumin, onion, bell pepper, chipotles, and sweet potatoes. Cover and cook on High for 2 minutes. Open and add the adobo sauce and frozen corn. Warm the corn and serve.

Taco Soup
Cook time:11 minutes| Serves: 4| Per serving: Calories 296; Carbs 39.7g; Fat 9.8g; Protein 15.2g

Ingredients:

- Red onion – 1, diced
- Garlic powder – 3 tbsps.
- Black beans – 1 large can, drained
- Diced tomatoes – 1 large can
- Tomato sauce – 1 large can
- Corn – 1 can
- Frozen chopped spinach – 1 cup
- Prepared rice – 1 cup
- Taco seasoning – 1 packet
- Salt and black pepper to taste
- Cilantro -1 tsp.

Directions:

Add everything in the Instant Pot and mix. Cover and cook on High for 3 minutes. Do a quick release. Let simmer uncovered on Sauté for 8 minutes. Serve.

Beans with Jalapenos
Cook time: 45 minutes |Serves: 3 | Per serving: Calories 61; Carbs 12.5g; Fat 1.3g; Protein 3.2g

Ingredients:

- Dry pinto beans – 1 ½ cups, rinsed
- Chili powder – 1 tbsp.
- Cumin – 1 tbsp.
- Salt – 1 tsp.
- Salsa – ¾ cups
- Diced jalapenos – 4 oz.
- Water as needed

Directions:

Place the beans in the Instant Pot. Add enough water, so the beans are submerged by 2-inches of water. Cook on High for 45 minutes. Place the drained beans in a bowl. Add salt, cumin and chili powder. With a hand mixture, blend until it reaches your desired consistency. Add diced jalapenos and salsa to the beans and mix well. Serve.

Lemon Ginger Asparagus
Cook time: 2 minutes| Serves: 4| Per serving: Calories 84; Carbs 5g; Fat 7g; Protein 3g

Ingredients:

- Asparagus – 1 bunch, tough ends removed
- Water – 1 cup
- Olive oil – 2 tbsps.
- Lemon juice – 1 tbsp.
- Salt – ½ to 1 tsp.
- Grated peeled fresh ginger – ½ tsp

Directions:

Add water to the Instant Pot. Place a steamer basket into the Instant Pot and add asparagus on top. Close and cook for 2 minutes. Do a quick release. In a bowl, stir together ginger, salt, lemon juice, and oil. Add the asparagus to the bowl. Toss and serve.

Slaw in Cups
Cook time: 8 minutes| Serves: 6| Per serving: Calories 344; Carbs 65g; Fat 5g; Protein 11g

Ingredients:

- Wonton or dumpling wrappers - 12
- Water – 1 cup
- Sliced green cabbage – 2 cups
- Shredded sweet potato – 1 cup
- Sweet onion – ½, sliced
- Lite soy sauce – 2 tbsps.
- Hoisin sauce – 1 tbsp.
- Lemon juice – 1 ½ tbsps.
- Sesame oil – 1 ½ tsps.
- Zest of 1 lime
- Ground ginger – ½ tsp. plus more to taste
- Scallions – 3, green and light green parts, sliced

Directions:

Preheat the oven. Use nonstick spray to coat a muffin tin. Place one wonton wrapper in each well of the prepared tin. Bake for 5 to 6 minutes. Set aside. Pour water into the Instant Pot. Place a steamer basket into the Instant Pot and place onion, sweet potato, and cabbage on the basket.

Cover, press Steam and cook for 2 minutes. Meanwhile, in a bowl, stir together the ginger, lime zest, lime juice, hoisin sauce, oil, and soy sauce. Open and stir in the veggies. Coat well. Before serving, fill the cups with the slaw and sprinkle the tops with scallion. Serve.

Creamy Corn
Cook time: 20 minutes| Serves: 4| Per serving: Calories 395; Carbs 44g; Fat 23g; Protein 12g

Ingredients:

- Raw cashews - 1 cup, soaked overnight and drained
- Vegetable stock – 1 cup
- Lemon juice – 2 tbsps.
- Sugar – 1 tbsp.
- Salt – 1 tsp. plus more for seasoning
- Vegetable oil – ½ tsp.
- Frozen sweet corn – 20 oz.
- Milk – ¾ cup
- Butter – 1 tbsp.
- Smoked paprika – ¼ tsp.
- Ground black pepper

Directions:

In a food processor, combine the oil, salt, sugar, lemon juice, stock, and cashews. Blend until smooth. Pour cashew mixture into the Instant Pot. Add paprika, butter, milk, and corn. Season with salt and pepper. Press Slow Cooker and cook 20 minutes. Remove the lid and stir the corn. Serve.

Cauliflower Veggie Mashup
Cook time: 10 minutes |Serves: 4 | Per serving: Calories 119; Carbs 12.7g; Fat 7.5g; Protein 3.5g

Ingredients:

- Carrots – 2
- Yellow zucchini – 1, chopped
- Cauliflower – 2 cups, chopped
- Broccoli – 1 cup, chopped
- Coconut milk – ½ cup
- Salt and pepper
- Red pepper – 1
- Parmesan cheese for garnishing

Directions:

Add everything in the Instant Pot and cover. Cook on High for 10 minutes. Do a natural release. Open and stir. Garnish with parmesan and serve.

Red Thai Curry Cauliflower

Cook time: 2 minutes| Serves: 4 | Per serving: Calories 349; Carbs 18g; Fat 31g; Protein 5g

Ingredients:

- Full-fat coconut milk – 1 (14-ounce) can
- Water – 1 cup
- Red curry paste – 2 tbsps.
- Garlic powder – 1 tsp.
- Salt – 1 tsp. plus more as needed
- Ground ginger – ½ tsp.
- Onion powder – ½ tsp.
- Chili powder – ¼ tsp.
- Bell pepper – 1, sliced
- Cauliflower – 1 medium head, chopped
- Diced tomatoes and liquid – 1 (14-ounce) can
- Freshly ground black pepper

Directions:

Stir together the chili powder, onion powder, ginger, salt, garlic powder, curry paste, water, and coconut milk in the Instant Pot. Mix. Add tomatoes, cauliflower, and bell pepper and mix. Cover and cook on High for 2 minutes. Open and stir. Taste and adjust seasoning. Serve.

Butternut Mac 'N' Cheese

Cook time: 2 minutes| Serves: 6| Per serving: Calories 520; Carbs 78g; Fat 14g; Protein 23g

Ingredients:

- Raw cashews – 1 cup, soaked overnight, drained and rinsed
- Cooked cubed butternut squash – 2 cups
- Nutritional yeast – 1/3 cup
- Lemon juice – 2 tbsps.
- Dijon mustard – 1 tsp.
- Salt – 2 tsp
- Ground nutmeg – 1/8 tsp
- Water – 4 ½ cups, divided
- Pasta – 1 (16-ounce) box
- Milk – 1 cup, plus more as needed
- Ground black pepper

Directions:

Combine 2 cups water, cashews, squash, nutritional yeast, lemon juice, mustard, salt, and nutmeg in a food processor and combine until smooth. Pour the mixture into the Instant Pot. Add the rest 2 ½ cups water into the blender and blend to capture any remaining mixture. Add to the Instant

Pot, and pasta. Cover and cook on Low for 2 minutes. Do a natural release. Remove the lid and stir in milk. Mix. Serve.

Broccoli Patties

Cook time: 5 minutes| Serves: 6| Per serving: Calories 79; Carbs 14.2g; Fat 1.7g; Protein 3.3g

Ingredients:

- Broccoli florets – 1 pound
- Wheat flour – 3 tbsps.
- Salt – 1 tsp.
- Fresh dill - 1 tbsp. chopped
- Potato – 1, peeled
- Red onion – ½, grated
- Olive oil – 1 tsp.
- Water - 1 cup for cooking

Directions:

Pour water in the Instant Pot and insert steamer rack. Place broccoli and potato on the steamer rack and close. Cook on High for 3 minutes. Then do a natural release. Transfer potato and broccoli to the blender. Add salt, fresh dill, grated onion, and blend until smooth. Then make medium patties from the mixture and coat them in wheat flour. Freeze the patties in the freezer for 10 minutes. Meanwhile, preheat the Instant Pot on Sauté and grease with olive oil. Place the frozen patties in the pot and close the lid. Cook on High for 2 minutes. Serve.

Sweet Potato Burgers

Cook time: 20 minutes| Serves: 2 | Per serving: Calories 139; Carbs 19.7g; Fat 6.4g; Protein 4.3g

Ingredients:

- Sweet potato – 1
- Onion – ½, diced
- Chives – 1 tsp.
- Salt – ½ tsp.
- Cayenne pepper – 1 tsp.
- Flax meal – 3 tbsps.
- Kale – ½ cup
- Olive oil - 1 tsp.
- Water – ½ cup, for cooking
- Burger buns – 2, cut into halves

Directions:

Pour water in the Instant Pot and insert steamer rack. Place sweet potato on the steamer rack and close the lid. Cook on High for 15 minutes and do a quick release. Meanwhile, place, onion, chives, and kale in the blender. Blend until smooth. Transfer the blended mixture into the mixing bowl. When the sweet potato is cooked, cut it into halves and scoop all the flesh into the kale mixture. Mix. Add flax meal, salt, and cayenne pepper. Stir well. Make medium burgers from the mixture. Clean the Instant Pot bowl and add olive oil. Preheat on Sauté for 2 to 3 minutes. Add burgers and cook for 2 minutes on each side. Serve with burger buns.

Black Bean Burger

Cook time: 5 minutes| Serves: 5| Per serving: Calories 155; Carbs 28.8g; Fat 1g; Protein 9.2g

Ingredients:

- Black beans – 1 cup, cooked
- Breadcrumbs – 2 tbsps.
- Salt – 1 tsp.
- Sweet corn – ¼ cup, cooked
- Turmeric – 1 tsp.
- Fresh parsley – 1 tbsp. chopped
- Yellow sweet pepper – ½, chopped
- Water – ½ cup
- Burger buns – 5, cut into halves

Directions:

Mash the black beans until they are puree and combine with salt, sweet corn, turmeric, parsley, and sweet pepper. Mix and add breadcrumbs. Mix again. Pour water into the Instant Pot and insert seamer rack. Make the burgers from the black bean mixture and freeze for 30 minutes. Wrap burgers in foil and place on the steamer rack. Close the lid and cook on High for 5 minutes. Do a natural release. Remove the foil from the burgers and transfer them to a plate. Serve with burger buns.

Seitan Burger

Cook time: 2 minutes| Serves: 1| Per serving: Calories 303; Carbs 24.9g; Fat 8.8g; Protein 26.8g

Ingredients:

- Burger bun – 1, cut into halves
- Mustard – 1 tsp.
- Soy sauce – 1 tsp.
- Seitan steak – 1
- Onion powder – 1 tsp.
- Olive oil - 1 tsp.
- Apple cider vinegar - 1 tbsp.

Directions:

Make the sauce for the seitan steak: mix up together soy sauce, onion powder, olive oil, and apple cider vinegar. Brush seitan steak with sauce on each side and place in the Instant Pot. Close the lid and cook on Manual for 2 minutes. Then do a quick release. Meanwhile, cut burger buns into halves and spread with mustard. Place seitan steak on the one-half of the burger bun and cover with the second one.

Apple Patties
Cook time: 6 minutes| Serves: 4| Per serving: Calories 104; Carbs 23.3g; Fat 1.4g; Protein 1g

Ingredients:

- Granny smith apples – 2
- Wheat flour – 3 tbsps.
- Baking powder – ½ tsp.
- Brown sugar - 1 tbsp.
- Vanilla extract – 1 tsp.
- Olive oil – 1 tsp.

Directions:

Grate the apples and place them in a bowl. Add wheat flour, baking powder, sugar, and vanilla extract. Mix and let it rest. Meanwhile, press Sauté and preheat the Instant Pot. Pour olive oil in the Instant Pot. Make patties from the apple mixture and put in the Instant Pot. Sauté the patties for 3 minutes on each side or until golden brown. Serve.

Zucchini Patties
Cook time: 5 minutes| Serves: 2 | Per serving: Calories 159; Carbs 26.2g; Fat 5g; Protein 5.6g

Ingredients:

- Zucchini – 1, grated
- Ground black pepper – ½ tsp.
- Smoked paprika – 1 tsp.
- Turmeric – ¼ tsp.
- Salt – 1 tsp.
- Flax meal – 3 Tbsps.
- Sesame seeds - 1 tsp.
- White rice – ¼ cup, boiled

Directions:

In a bowl, mix grated zucchini, ground black pepper, smoked paprika, and turmeric. Add salt, flax meal, sesame seeds, and boiled rice. Mix the mixture and make patties. Freeze the patties in the freezer for 20 minutes. Wrap the frozen patties in the foil and place them on the steamer rack. Insert the rack into the Instant Pot and close the lid. Cook patties for 5 minutes on High. Do a quick release. Remove foil from the patties and serve.

Pumpkin Burger

Cook time: 3 minutes| Serves: 2| Per serving: Calories 197; Carbs 30.5g; Fat 5.6g; Protein 7.2g

Ingredients:

- Hamburger buns – 2
- Pumpkin seeds – 1 tbsp.
- Pumpkin powder – 1 tbsp.
- Pumpkin pure – 3 tbsps.
- Breadcrumbs – 2 tbsps.
- Chili flakes – ½ tsp.
- Turmeric - 1 tsp.
- Flax meal - 1 tbsp.
- Hot water – 3 tbsps.

Directions:

In a bowl, mix flax meal and water. Whisk the mixture and add the pumpkin powder, pumpkin puree, breadcrumbs, chili flakes, and turmeric. Mix and add pumpkin seeds. Make 2 burgers. Place them in the Instant Pot and close the lid. Cook on High for 3 minutes. Do a quick release and open the lid. Fill the burger buns with pumpkin burgers. Serve.

Pumpkin Cream Soup

Cook time: 20 minutes| Serves: 5| Per serving: Calories 305; Carbs 24.8g; Fat 23.4g; Protein 4.8g

Ingredients:

- Coconut cream - 2 cups
- Water – 2 cups
- Pumpkin – 3 cups, chopped
- Salt – 1 tsp.
- Paprika – 1 tsp.
- Ground cardamom – ¼ tsp.
- Turmeric – ½ tsp.
- Potato – 1, peeled
- Wheat flour – 1 tbsp.

Directions:

Whisk water with wheat flour until smooth and pour mixture in the Instant Pot. Add chopped pumpkin, coconut cream, salt, paprika, ground cardamom, and turmeric. Grate the potato and add it in the Instant Pot. Close and cook on High for 20 minutes. Do a quick release and open. Blend with a hand mixer and serve.

Cauliflower Soup

Cook time: 15 minutes| Serves: 4| Per serving: Calories 106; Carbs 9.7g; Fat 7.3g; Protein 3g

Ingredients:

- Cauliflower head – 1 pound
- Coconut cream – ¼ cup
- Water – 2 cups
- Lemon juice – 2 tbsps.
- Olive oil – 1 tbsp.
- Onion – 1, diced
- Salt – 1 tsp.
- Ground black pepper – ½ tsp.
- Water – ½ cup, for cooking

Directions:

Pour ½ cup water in the Instant Pot and insert steamer rack. Place cauliflower on the rack and close the lid. Cook on High for 5 minutes, then do a quick release. Remove cauliflower and water from the Instant Pot. Pour water in the Instant Pot. Add diced onion and sauté for 3 to 4 minutes. Sprinkle the onion with salt and ground black pepper. Chop cooked cauliflower and add into the Instant Pot. Then add water and coconut cream. Close and seal the lid. Cook on High for 4 minutes. Do a quick release and open the lid. Blend the soup with a hand mixer. Ladle the soup in the bowls and sprinkle with lemon juice. Serve.

French Onion Soup

Cook time: 25 minutes |Serves: 2| Per serving: Calories 332; Carbs 27.7g ; Fat 14g ; Protein 19.5g

Ingredients:

- Onion – 3 cups, diced
- Coconut oil – 2 tbsps.
- Water - ¼ cup
- Vegetable broth – 2 cups
- Salt – 1 tsp.
- Ground black pepper – 1 tsp.
- Minced garlic – 1 tsp.
- Ground nutmeg - ½ tsp.
- Parmesan – 3 oz. grated

Directions:

Add oil and onions in the Instant Pot and cook on Sauté for 3 to 4 minutes. Add salt, ground black pepper, minced garlic, and ground nutmeg. Stir well. When the onions start to become tender, add water and mix. Close the lid and cook on High for 12 minutes. Then do a quick release. Add broth and mix. Close the lid and cook on Sauté for 10 minutes more. Top with parmesan and serve.

Lentil Soup

Cook time: 15 minutes| Serves: 2| Per serving: Calories 349; Carbs 57.3g; Fat 11g; Protein 27.3g

Ingredients:

- Red lentils – 1 cup
- Potato – 1, chopped
- Onion – ½, chopped
- Water – 5 cups
- Salt – 1 tsp.
- Ground black pepper – 1 tsp.
- Coconut oil – 1 tbsp.
- Chili flakes - 1 tsp.
- Tomato paste – 1 tbsp.

Directions:

Melt coconut oil in the Instant Pot on Sauté. Add onion and potato and sauté for 7 minutes. Add salt, ground black pepper, chili flakes, and tomato paste. Mix and add the lentils. Add the water and mix again. Close the lid. Cook on High for 8 minutes. Do a natural release and serve.

Vegetable Stew

Cook time: 45 minutes| Serves: 2| Per serving: Calories 100; Carbs 22.4 g; Fat 1.2g; Protein 3g

Ingredients:

- Yellow onion – ½ chopped
- Celery stalk – 1 oz. chopped
- Carrot – ¼ cup, chopped
- Garlic – 1 clove, chopped
- Tomato sauce – 1 tbsp.
- Green peas – ¼ cup
- Tomato – 1, chopped
- Vegetable stock – 1 cup
- Salt – 1 tsp.
- Thyme – 1 tsp.
- Yukon potatoes – 2, chopped

Directions:

Add the potatoes, celery, yellow onion, carrot, garlic, tomato sauce, green peas, tomato, salt, thyme, and mix. Add the vegetable stock and close the lid. Press Sauté and cook for 45 minutes on High. Open mix and serve.

Peas and Carrot Stew

Cook time: 10 minutes | Serves: 5 | Per serving: Calories 125; Carbs 27.5g; Fat 0.3g; Protein 4.1g

Ingredients:

- Potatoes – 3, peeled and chopped
- Carrots – 2, chopped
- Green peas – 1 cup, frozen
- Water – 2 cups
- Tomato paste – 1 tbsp.
- Salt – 1 tsp.
- Cayenne pepper – 1 tsp.

Directions:

Place the potatoes, carrots, and green peas in the Instant Pot. Then in a bowl, combine tomato paste, water, salt, and cayenne pepper. Whisk the liquid and then pour it into the Instant Pot. Close the lid and cook on High for 10 minutes. Do a natural release and serve.

Sweet Potato Stew II

Cook time: 35 minutes | Serves: 2 | Per serving: Calories 165; Carbs 24.7g; Fat 7.4g; Protein 2.6g

Ingredients:

- Tomatoes – ¼ cup, diced
- Wheat flour – 1 tbsp.
- Tomato juice – 1 cup
- Onion – ½, chopped
- Olive oil – 1 tbsp.
- Chives – 1 tbsp. chopped
- Salt – 1 tsp.
- Curry powder – 1 tsp.
- Sweet potatoes – 3, chopped
- Water – ½ cup
- Brown sugar – 1 tsp.

Directions:

Pour olive oil in the Instant Pot. Add onion and sweet potatoes. Add salt, curry powder, and cook on Sauté for 10 minutes. In a bowl, whisk together wheat flour and water until smooth. Pour the liquid in the Instant Pot. Add tomato juice and sugar. Close the lid and cook on Sauté for 35 minutes. Mix the stew every 10 minutes. Serve.

Turkish Green Beans

Cook time: 15 minutes| Serves: 4| Per serving: Calories 61; Carbs 6.9g; Fat 3.7g; Protein 1.5g

Ingredients:

- Green beans – 1 ½ cup, chopped
- Onion – ½, diced
- Tomatoes – 2, chopped
- Tomato paste – 1 tsp.
- Chili flakes – 1 tsp.
- Salt – 1 tsp.
- Water – 1 cup
- Olive oil – 1 tbsp.

Directions:

Add oil, onion, and green beans in the Instant Pot. Stir-fry on Sauté for 5 minutes. Add salt, chili flakes, tomato paste, and water. Close the lid and cook on High for 8 minutes. Do a natural release and open. Mix and serve.

Lentil Gumbo

Cook time: 23 minutes| Serves: 4| Per serving: Calories 129; Carbs 20.7g; Fat 2.2g; Protein 7.7g

Ingredients:

- Garlic – ½ tbsp. diced
- Coconut oil – ½ tbsp.
- Bell pepper – 1, chopped
- Celery – 1 stalk, chopped
- Thyme – ½ tsp.
- Coriander – 1½ tsps.
- Cajun spices – 1 tsp.
- White pepper – ½ tsp.
- Lentils - ½ cup
- Water – 1 ½ cup
- Okra – ½ cup, chopped
- Tomatoes – ½ cup, diced, canned
- Lemon juice – 1 tsp.
- Cauliflower – 4 oz. chopped
- Salt – 1 tsp.

Directions:

Preheat the Instant Pot on Sauté and add oil. Add bell pepper, garlic, celery stalk, thyme, coriander, and Cajun spices. Mix and cook for 10 minutes. Then add everything except the salt. Close the lid and cook on High for 13 minutes. Do a quick release. Open and add salt. Serve.

Chapter 7 Poultry Recipes

Kung Pao Chicken
Cook time: 17 minutes | Serves: 5| Per serving: Calories 380; Carbs 7g; Fat 25g; Protein 30.6g

Ingredients:

- Coconut oil – 2 tbsps.
- Boneless, skinless chicken breasts – 1 pound, cubed
- Hot sauce – 6 tbsps.
- Cashews – ½ cup, chopped
- Ginger – ½ tsp. finely grated
- Chili powder – ½ tsp.
- Kosher salt – ½ tsp.
- Freshly ground black pepper – ½ tsp.

Directions:

Press Sauté add oil and heat it. Add chicken, salt, pepper, chili powder, ginger, cashews, and hot sauce. Close the lid and Press Manual. Cook on High for 17 minutes.

Chicken Cacciatore
Cook time: 18 minutes| Serves: 4 | Per serving: Calories 344; Carbs 5g; Fat 24.3g; Protein 26.5g

Ingredients:

- Coconut oil – 6 tbsps.
- Chicken legs – 5
- Bell pepper – 1, diced
- Dried basil – ½ tsp.
- Onion – ½, chopped
- Dried parsley – ½ tsp.
- Salt – ½ tsp.
- Freshly ground black pepper – ½ tsp.
- Diced tomatoes – 1 (14-ounce) can

Directions:

Press Sauté and melt the oil. Add the chicken and sauté until browned. Remove chicken and set aside. Add tomatoes, black pepper, salt, parsley, onion, basil, and pepper and sauté. Add ½-cup water and add the chicken on top. Close the lid and hit Cancel. Press Manual and cook on High for 18 minutes. Do a natural release and serve.

Chicken Casserole

Cook time: 20 minutes| Serves: 4|Per serving: Calories 538; Carbs 4.9g; Fat 30.8g; Protein 57.9g

Ingredients:

- Pepperoni – 16 slices, uncured
- Mozzarella cheese – 1 cup, shredded
- Full-fat cheddar cheese – 1 cup, shredded
- Chicken – 1 pound, ground
- Egg – 1
- Garlic – 1 tsp. minced
- Full-fat Parmesan cheese – ½ cup, grated
- Dried parsley – ½ tsp.
- Thyme – ½ tsp.
- Dried basil – ½ tsp.
- Black pepper - ½ tsp.
- Crushed red pepper – ½ tsp.
- Dried oregano – ½ tsp.
- Fire roasted tomatoes – 1 (14 ounces) can

Directions:

Add 1-cup water into the Instant Pot. Insert the trivet. In a bowl, combine tomatoes, oregano, red pepper, black pepper, basil, thyme, parsley, Parmesan, garlic, egg, chicken, cheddar, mozzarella, and pepperoni slices. Mix well and transfer mixture into a greased dish. Place the dish on top of the trivet. Use an aluminum foil to cover loosely. Close the lid and press Manual. Cook 20 minutes on High. Do a natural release and open. Serve.

Spicy Turkey Meatballs

Cook time: 25 minutes| Serves: 5 |Per serving: Calories 205; Carbs 0.7g; Fat 10.1g; Protein 26.7 g

Ingredients:

- Ground turkey – 1 pound
- Hot sauce – ¼ cup
- Coconut oil – 2 tbsps.
- Grated ginger – 1 tsp.
- Chili powder – ½ tsp.
- Basil – ½ tsp. dried
- Salt – ½ tsp.
- Ground black pepper – ½ tsp.

Directions:

Make 1 ½ inch meatballs with the ground turkey and place in a dish. In a bowl, stir together salt, pepper, basil, chili powder, ginger, oil, and hot sauce. Mix and sprinkle evenly over the meatballs.

Add 1 cup water into the Instant Pot and insert the trivet. Gently place the meatball dish on top of the trivet. Close and press Manual. Cook 25 minutes on high. Do a natural pressure release. Open and serve.

Salsa Verde Chicken

Cook time: 25 minutes| Serves: 6| Per serving: Calories 340; Carbs 5g; Fat 6.8g; Protein 55g

Ingredients:

- Salsa Verde – 16 ounces
- Chicken breasts – 2 ½ pounds
- Cumin – 1 tsp.
- Garlic powder – ¼ tsp.
- Salt – 1 tsp.
- Pepper – ¼ tsp.
- Pinch of paprika

Directions:

Whisk together the salsa and spices in the Instant Pot. Add the chicken. Close the lid and press the Manual. Cook for 25 minutes on High. Do a quick pressure release. Serve.

Italian Duck with Spinach

Cook time: 15 minutes| Serves: 3| Per serving: Calories 455; Carbs 1g; Fat 26g; Protein 57g

Ingredients:

- Duck breasts – 1 pound, halved
- Spinach – ½ cup, chopped
- Chopped Sun-Dried Tomatoes – ¼ cup
- Chicken stock – ½ cup
- Grated Parmesan Cheese – ¼ cup
- Italian seasoning – 1 tsp.
- Heavy cream – 1/3 cup
- Minced garlic – 1 tsp.
- Salt and pepper to taste
- Olive oil – 2 tbsps.

Directions:

Whisk together the seasoning, garlic, oil, and salt and pepper. Rub this mixture into the meat. Place the duck in the IP and cook on Sauté until golden on all sides. Add the stock, close the lid and cook on Manual for 4 minutes. Press Cancel and do a quick release. Stir in the remaining ingredients and cover. Cook on High for 5 minutes more. Release the pressure quickly and serve.

Soft and Juicy Chicken

Cook time: 30 minutes| Serves: 10| Per serving: Calories 270; Carbs 3g; Fat 20g; Protein 22g

Ingredients:

- Chicken – 1 (4-pound)
- Coconut oil – 1 tbsp.
- Lemon juice – 2 tbsps.
- Garlic – 2 cloves, peeled
- Paprika – 1 tsp.
- Chicken stock – 1 ½ cups
- Salt – ½ tsp.
- Pepper – ¼ tsp.
- Onion powder – 1 tsp.

Directions:

In a bowl, combine all the spices. Rub the mixture into the chicken. Add the coconut oil in the IP and melt on Sauté. Add the chicken and cook until browned on all sides. Pour the stock and lemon juice over. Add the garlic cloves. Close and cook on Manual for 25 minutes. Serve.

Chicken Bowl with Pine Nuts

Cook time:20 minutes| Serves: 4|Per serving: Calories 328; Carbs 11.1g; Fat 20.6g; Protein 24.7g

Ingredients:

- Chicken legs – 1 pound, skinless and cut into pieces
- Olive oil – 1 tbsp.
- Red wine vinegar – 2 tbsps.
- Watercress – 1-ounce, tough stalks removed and chopped
- Bell pepper – 1, chopped
- Sweet onion – 1, sliced
- Garlic – 2 cloves, minced
- Cucumber – 1, sliced
- Gem lettuce – 2 cups, leaves separated
- Ground black pepper and salt to taste
- Spanish paprika – 1 tsp.
- Marjoram – ½ tsp.
- Oregano – ½ tsp.
- Pine nuts – 4 tbsps.
- Water – 1 cup, for the pot

Directions:

Add 1 cup water and a metal rack to the Instant Pot. Lower the chicken legs onto the metal rack. Cover and cook on Steam mode for 15 minutes on High. Do a quick release and open. Slice the chicken into bite-sized pieces and discard the bones. Place the meat into a bowl. Clean the Instant Pot and add 1 tbsp. oil. Heat on Sauté. Add sweet onion and garlic and sauté for 5 minutes. Add the remaining ingredients except for the pine nuts and lettuce and mix. Add the mixture to the bowl and toss to combine. Garnish with pine nuts and serve with lettuce leaves.

Greek Chicken and Rice

Cook time: 4 minutes |Serves: 4| Per serving: Calories 314.3; Carbs 31.4g; Fat 9g; Protein 26.7g

Ingredients:

- Rice – 1 cup
- Chicken breasts – 3, diced
- Red bell pepper – 1, chopped
- Yellow bell pepper – 1, chopped
- Zucchini – 1, sliced
- Red onion – 1, chopped
- Minced garlic – 2 tsps.
- Salt – ½ tsp.
- Ground black pepper – ½ tsp.
- Oregano – 1 tbsp.
- Lemon juice – 3 tbsps.
- Olive oil – 2 tbsps.
- Chicken broth – 1 ½ cups
- Parsley – ¼ cup, chopped
- Feta cheese – ¼ cup, crumbled

Directions:

Add everything in the Instant Pot except for zucchini, peppers, cheese, and parsley. Mix and cover the pot. Cook for 4 minutes on High. Do a natural release and open. Stir in chicken and remaining ingredients. Close and let rest for 10 minutes. Top with cheese and serve.

Turkey Cheese Gnocchi

Cook time: 25 minutes|Serves:6| Per serving: Calories 533; Carbs 32.6g; Fat 19.9g; Protein 99.2g

Ingredients:

- Turkey boneless pieces – 1 pound
- Fresh spinach – 2 cups, chopped
- Mozzarella cheese – 2 cups, shredded
- Parmesan cheese – ½ cup, shredded
- Olive oil – 2 tbsps.
- Black pepper – ½ tsp.

- Shallots – ¼ cup, chopped
- Garlic minced – 2 cloves
- Sun-dried tomatoes – ¼ cup, chopped
- Cream – 1 cup
- Chicken broth – 2 cups
- Gnocchi – 2 lbs.
- Salt – ½ tsp.

Directions:

Press Sauté and then add the oil. Add the turkey with salt and pepper. Cook 3 minutes on each side. Add the garlic, tomatoes, and shallots to the pot. Cook and stir for 2 minutes. Add the cream and chicken broth to the pot. Cover the pot. Cook on High for 10 minutes, then do a natural release. Add gnocchi to the mixture and press Sauté. Cook for 5 minutes, or until gnocchi is tender. Add cheese and serve.

Chicken with Smoked Paprika

Cook time:20 minutes|Serves:6 |Per serving: Calories 524; Carbs 29.3g; Fat 10.3g; Protein 68.5g

Ingredients:

- Chicken breasts – 1 ½ lb. cut into small pieces
- Smoked paprika – 2 tsps.
- Olive oil – 1 tsp.
- Bacon – 3 strips, chopped
- Onion – 1, chopped
- Garlic – 2 cloves, minced
- Red bell pepper – 1, chopped
- Salt – ½ tsp.
- Beer – 1 (12 oz.) can
- White rice – 1 cup
- Bacon – 2 strips, cooked (topping)

Directions:

Put the oil and bacon in the pot. Sauté for 3 minutes. Add the bell pepper and stir-fry for 3 minutes more. Add chopped onion and cook for 2 minutes. Add garlic and cook for 1 minute. Add all the seasoning to the pot and add the beer. Mix. Add the chicken and rice and cover the pot. Cook on High for 10 minutes. Do a quick release and open. Serve dish topped with bacon.

Turkey Noodle Soup

Cook time: 40 minutes| Serves: 4| Per serving: Calories 358; Carbs 9.4g; Fat 11.6g; Protein 56.7g

Ingredients:

For the broth

- Shredded turkey – 1 cup
- Turkey carcass – 1, left over from a carved turkey
- Water – 14 cups
- Onion – 1, chopped
- Carrots -3, chopped
- Celery – 2 stalks, chopped
- Salt and pepper to taste

Soup

- Cooked turkey meat – 3 cups, chopped
- Cooked egg noodles – 8 oz.
- Scallions – 4, chopped
- Salt and pepper to taste

Directions:

Put the water, onion, celery, carrots, salt, pepper, and turkey pieces into the Instant Pot. Cover and cook on Soup function, on High for 35 minutes. Do a natural release and open. Strain the broth and put the broth back into the pot. Add the shredded turkey, carrots, and celery. Press Sauté and boil the soup. Add the cooked noodles and cook for 1 minute more. Serve with scallions for garnishing.

Duck Breast with Prosciutto

Cook time: 27 minutes| Serves:4 |Per serving: Calories 496; Carbs 3.5g; Fat 34.3g; Protein 40.9g

Ingredients:

- Duck breasts – 1 lb.
- Shallot – 1, finely chopped
- Garlic cloves – 2, crushed
- Duck fat – ½ cup
- Chicken broth – 4 cups
- Prosciutto – 7 oz. chopped
- Fresh parsley – 2 tbsps. finely chopped
- Apple cider vinegar – 3 tbsps.
- Cremini mushrooms – 1 cup
- Orange zest – 1 tbsp.
- Sea salt – 1 tsp.

- White pepper – ½ tsp. freshly ground

Directions:

Press Sauté and add duck fat. Stir constantly and slowly melt the fat. Add the garlic and shallots. Cook and stir for 2 to 3 minutes. Add the mushrooms and continue to cook until the liquid has evaporated. Add the prosciutto and stir well. Briefly brown on all sides and press Cancel. Add the meat in the pot and pour in the broth. Sprinkle with orange zest and spices. Pour in the cider and seal the lid. Press Manual and cook 20 minutes on High pressure. Once cooked release pressure naturally and open the lid. Sprinkle with parsley and cover for 10 minutes before serving.

Salsa Verde Turkey Breast

Cook time: 30 minutes| Serves: 4| Per serving: Calories 342; Carbs 5.5g; Fat 17.7g; Protein 37.8g

Ingredients:

- Medium sized turkey breast – 2, cut in half
- Onion – 1, sliced
- Chicken broth – 3 cups

For the salsa Verde

- Tomatillos – 1 cup, chopped
- Fresh parsley – ¼ cup, finely chopped
- Green chili – 1, finely chopped
- Onion powder – 1 tsp.
- Garlic cloves – 2, crushed
- Olive oil – 3 tbsps.
- Salt – 1 tsp.
- Chili powder – ¼ tsp.

For the rub

- Chili powder – 1 tsp.
- Garlic powder – 2 tsps.
- Onion powder – 1 tsp.
- Salt – 1 tsp.
- Cumin powder – ½ tsp.

Directions:

Combine garlic powder, chili powder, onion powder, salt and cumin in a bowl. Mix well and set aside. Rub the meat with the spices. Place at the bottom of the IP and pour in the chicken broth. Add onions and seal the lid. Press Poultry and cook on High for 15 minutes. When cooked, remove the meat from the pot and set aside. Remove broth and press Sauté. Grease the inner pot with olive oil and heat up. Add garlic and green chili. Cook for 2 to 3 minutes and then add the tomatillos along with the remaining ingredients for the salsa. Pour in about 3 tbsps. of the broth and simmer for 10 to 12 minutes. Stirring occasionally. Press Cancel and remove the mixture from the pot. Transfer to a food processor and process until smooth. Drizzle over the meat and serve.

Italian Chicken Thighs

Cook time: 17 minutes |Serves: 6| Per serving: Calories 245; Carbs 7g; Fat 25g; Protein 35g

Ingredients:

- Chicken thighs – 6
- Cherry tomatoes – 2 cups
- Basil – ½ cup
- Garlic – 3 cloves, minced
- Onion – 1, chopped
- Cremini mushrooms – ½ pound, sliced
- Olives – ½ cup
- Tomato paste – 1 tbsp.
- Olive oil – 1 tbsp.
- Parsley – ¼ cup
- Chicken broth – 1 cup

Directions:

Heat the olive oil in your IP on Sauté. Sear the chicken until golden. Set aside. Add onions and mushrooms and cook for a few minutes. Add garlic and cook for 30 seconds. Stir in the remaining ingredients including the chicken and close the lid. Cook on High for 10 minutes. Do a quick pressure release. Serve.

Glazed Duck Breast

Cook time: 25 minutes |Serves: 2| Per serving: Calories 398; Carbs 4.7g; Fat 15g; Protein 55.7g

Ingredients:

- Duck breast – 1 lb. chopped into bite-sized pieces, thaw if frozen
- Olive oil – 1 tbsp.
- Chicken broth – 3 cups
- Dijon mustard – 1 tbsp.
- Erythritol – 1 tsp. powdered
- Apple cider vinegar – ¼ cup
- Salt – 1 tsp.
- Pepper – ½ tsp.
- Garlic powder – 1 tsp.

Directions:

Rub the meat with garlic powder and place in the IP along with chicken broth. Seal the lid and press the Meat button. Once cooked, do a quick release and open the lid. Remove the meat from the pot along with the broth. Press the Sauté button and grease the insert with oil. Add erythritol, Dijon, and apple cider. Sprinkle with salt and pepper and cook for 3 to 4 minutes. Add the meat and coat well. Serve.

Chicken and Corn Soup

Cook time: 15 minutes| Serves: 4| Per serving: Calories 273; Carbs 6g; Fat 14g; Protein 18g

Ingredients:

- Oil – 2 tbsps.
- Yellow onion – ¼ cup, chopped
- Garlic – 1 tsp. minced
- Red bell pepper – ½ cup, chopped
- Chicken stock – 30 ounces, low sodium
- Chicken breasts – 1 ½ pounds, skinless, boneless and cubed
- Canned corn – 20 ounces, drained
- Tomatoes – 1 cup, chopped
- Chili powder – 1 tbsp.
- Coconut cream - 1 cup

Directions:

Heat the oil on Sauté. Add meat, onion, bell pepper and garlic. Cook for 3 minutes. Add the rest of the ingredients except the cream. Mix and cover. Cook on High for 10 minutes. Open and press Sauté. Add cream, stir and cook for 2 minutes. Serve.

Chicken and Pea Soup

Cook time: 20 minutes |Serves: 4| Per serving: Calories 192; Carbs 7g; Fat 5g; Protein 16g

Ingredients:

- Olive oil – 2 tbsps.
- Chicken breasts – 1 pound, skinless, boneless, and cubed
- Yellow onion – 1, chopped
- Carrots – ½ cup, chopped
- Garlic – 2 cloves, chopped
- Chicken stock – 28 ounces
- Salt and pepper to taste
- Fresh peas – 1 pounds
- Coconut cream – ½ cup
- Dill – 1 tbsp. chopped

Directions:

Heat oil on Sauté. Add chicken, onion, and garlic and brown for 4 minutes. add the rest of the ingredients except the cream and dill. Cover and cook on High for 12 minutes. Open and press Sauté. Add the cream and dill. Cook for 4 minutes and serve.

Chicken and Rice Soup

Cook time: 15 minutes| Serves: 4| Per serving: Calories 200; Carbs 6g; Fat 8g; Protein 12g

Ingredients:

- Yellow onion – 1, chopped
- Olive oil – 2 tbsps.
- Carrots – 1 cup, chopped
- Chicken stock – 28 ounces
- Chicken breasts – 2, skinless, boneless and cubed
- Wild rice – 6 ounces
- Salt and pepper to taste
- Parsley – 1 tbsp. chopped

Directions:

Heat oil on Sauté. Add chicken, onion, and carrots. Cook for 3 minutes. Add the rest of the ingredients except the parsley. Cover and cook on High for 12 minutes. Open and add parsley. Serve.

Turkey Salad

Cook time: 15 minutes| Serves: 4| Per serving: Calories 181; Carbs 7g; Fat 4g; Protein 15g

Ingredients:

- Turkey breast – 1 ½ pounds, skinless, boneless and cubed
- Tomatoes – 2, cubed
- Red bell peppers – 2, cut into strips
- Olive oil – 1 tbsp.
- Red onions – 2, chopped
- Parsley – ½ cup, chopped
- Canned tomatoes – 20 ounces, chopped
- Basil – 1 tbsp. chopped
- Salt and pepper to taste
- Baby arugula – 1 cup
- Baby spinach – ½ cup

Directions:

Heat oil on Sauté. Add onions and turkey and cook for 5 minutes. Add rest of the ingredients except for the basil, arugula and spinach and cover. Cook on High for 10 minutes. Open and add spinach, basil and arugula. Serve.

Turkey and Eggplant Mix

Cook time: 20 minutes |Serves: 4| Per serving: Calories 252; Carbs 7g; Fat 12g; Protein 13g

Ingredients:

- Big turkey breast – 1, skinless, boneless and cubed
- Salt and pepper to taste

- Big eggplant – 1, chopped
- Oil – 2 tbsps.
- Red onion – 1, chopped
- Tomato sauce – 10 ounces
- Oregano – 1 tbsp. dried
- Basil – 1 tsp. dried

Directions:

Heat oil on Sauté. Add onion and turkey and cook for 5 minutes. Add the rest of the ingredients and cover. Cook 15 minutes on High. Serve.

Lemongrass Turkey
Cook time: 25 minutes |Serves: 4| Per serving: Calories 263; Carbs 6g; Fat 12g; Protein 14g

Ingredients:

- Lemongrass – 1 bunch, chopped
- Garlic – 4 cloves, minced
- Balsamic vinegar – 2 tbsps.
- Oregano – 1 tbsp. chopped
- Coconut milk – 1 cup
- Turkey breasts – 2, skinless, boneless and cubed
- Salt and pepper to taste
- Cilantro – ¼ cup, chopped

Directions:

In a food processor, add everything except the turkey and milk and mix well. In the IP, combine the turkey with the lemongrass mix, and milk. Cover and cook on High for 25 minutes. Open and serve topped with cilantro.

Duck Curry
Cook time: 30 minutes| Serves: 4 | Per serving: Calories 231; Carbs 7g; Fat 12g; Protein 15g

Ingredients:

- Duck breasts – 1 ½ pounds, skinless, boneless and cubed
- Olive oil – 1 tbsp.
- Yellow onion – 1, sliced
- Canned coconut milk – 5 ounces
- Green curry paste – 1 tbsp.
- Coriander – ½ bunch, chopped

Directions:

Heat oil on Sauté. Add onion, curry paste and duck and cook for 5 minutes. Add the resto of the ingredients and cover. Cook on High for 25 minutes. Open and serve.

Parmesan Duck Breast

Cook time: 25 minutes| Serves: 4| Per serving: Calories 242; Carbs 7g; Fat 14g; Protein 14g

Ingredients:

- Olive oil – 1 tbsp.
- Duck breasts – 2 pounds, skinless, and boneless
- Salt and pepper to taste
- Chicken stock – 1 cup
- Yellow onion – 1, chopped
- Tomato – 1, cubed
- Parmesan cheese – 1 cup, shredded

Directions:

Heat oil on Sauté. Add onion and duck and cook for 5 minutes. Add everything except for the cheese and cover. Cook on High for 20 minutes. Open and sprinkle with cheese. Serve.

Duck and Rice Mix

Cook time: 30 minutes| Serves: 4 | Per serving: Calories 251; Carbs 7g; Fat 17g; Protein 14g

Ingredients:

- Ginger – 1 tbsp. grated
- Garlic – 4 cloves, minced
- Coconut milk – 1 cup
- Wild rice – 1 cup
- Chicken stock – 3 cups
- Duck breasts – 2, skinless, boneless and cubed
- Five spice – 1 tsp.
- Salt and pepper to taste
- Capers – 1 tbsp. drained and chopped

Directions:

Mix the duck with everything in the Pot. Cover and cook on High for 30 minutes. Open and serve.

Duck and Lentils

Cook time: 25 minutes| Serves: 4| Per serving: Calories 273; Carbs 6g; Fat 12g; Protein 13g

Ingredients:

- Duck – 2 breasts, boneless, halved and skin scored
- Red onion – 1, chopped
- Olive oil - 2 tbsps.
- Lentils – 8 ounces
- Parsley – 1 tbsp. chopped
- Chicken stock – 3 cups
- Salt and pepper to taste

Directions:

Heat oil on Sauté. Add onion and duck, skin side down and cook for 5 minutes. Add everything and cover. Cook on High for 20 minutes. Serve.

Chapter 8 Pork Recipes

Chinese Pork Soup
Cook time: 30 minutes| Serves: 5| Per serving: Calories 234; Carbs 2.3g; Fat 7.2g; Protein 29.3g

Ingredients:

- Olive oil – 1 tbsp.
- Ground pork – 1 pound
- Small yellow onion – 1 chopped
- Carrots – 2 cups, chopped
- Chopped cabbage – ½ head
- Homemade chicken broth – 4 cups
- Liquid aminos – ¼ cup
- Ground ginger – 1 tsp.
- Freshly ground black pepper to taste

Directions:

Place the oil in the Instant Pot and press Sauté. Add the pork and cook for 5 minutes. Add the remaining ingredients. Cover and cook on High pressure for 25 minutes. Serve.

Pork Chops
Cook time: 30 minutes |Serves: 4| Per serving: Calories 232; Carbs 0.8g; Fat 19.9g; Protein 12.2g

Ingredients:

- Coconut oil – 2 tbsps.
- Pork chops – 4, boneless
- Butter – 1 tbsp.
- Crushed red pepper – 1 tsp.
- Dried parsley – ½ tsp.
- Garlic powder – ½ tsp.
- Chili powder – ½ tsp.
- Dried basil – ½ tsp.
- Salt – ½ tsp.
- Ground black pepper – ½ tsp.
- Hot sauce – ¼ cup
- Water – 1 cup

Directions:

Press Sauté and melt the oil in the Instant Pot. Add pork chops and brown on both sides. Add 1-cup water, butter, black pepper, salt, basil, chili powder, garlic powder, parsley, and red pepper.

Close and cook 30 minutes on High. Do a natural release. Open the pork chops and rub with hot sauce. Serve.

Cinnamon Pork

Cook time: 15 minutes |Serves: 4| Per serving: Calories 543; Carbs 6g; Fat 36g; Protein 54g

Ingredients:

- Pork – 2 pounds, ground
- Pepper – ¼ tsp.
- Cinnamon – ½ tsp.
- Sweetener – 2 tbsps.
- Grated ginger – ½ tsp.
- Dijon mustard – 2 tbsps.
- Chicken broth – 1 cup
- Olive oil – 1 tbsp.
- Salt – ½ tsp.

Directions:

Season the meat with salt and pepper. Press Sauté and add oil to the Instant Pot. Add the meat and stir-fry until browned. Add the other ingredients and mix well. Close and cook 15 minutes on High. Do a quick release when done. Open and serve.

Ginger Pork

Cook time: 42 minutes| Serves: 3 | Per serving: Calories 576; Carbs 2.9g; Fat 24g; Protein 82.7g

Ingredients:

- Pork loin – 2 lbs. chopped into bite-size pieces.
- Eggplant – 1 cup, chopped
- Ghee – 3 tbsps.
- Spring onion – 1, finely chopped
- Garlic cloves – 3
- Beef stock – 3 cups
- Light soy sauce – 2 tbsps.
- Anka sauce – 1 tbsp.
- Balsamic vinegar – 1 tbsp.
- Ginger powder – 2 tsps.
- Anise star – 1
- Cloves – 3
- Sea salt – 2

Directions:

Place the meat at the bottom and add enough water to cover. Press Sauté and bring it to a boil. Cook for 5 minutes and stirring occasionally. Remove from the pot and drain. Set aside. Now grease the inner pot with ghee and heat up. Add cloves, anise, ginger powder and spring onions.

Simmer and stir for 1 minute. Add the anka sauce and cook for another minute. Add the meat and mix well. Add the rest of the ingredients. Cover and cook for 35 minutes on high. When done, do a quick pressure release and open the lid. Serve.

Chinese Pulled Pork

Cook time: 1 hour| Serves: 6| Per serving: Calories 459; Carbs 3g; Fat 35g; Protein 30g

Ingredients:

- Pork shoulder – 2 lbs.
- Chicken broth – 1 cup
- Tomato sauce – 4 tbsps.
- Tomato paste – 1 tbsp.
- Garlic paste – 2 tbsps.
- Soy sauce – 4 tbsps.
- Liquid sweetener – 5 drops
- Grated ginger – 2 tsps.
- Smoked paprika – 1 tsp.

Directions:

Except for pork, place all the ingredients in a bowl and mix well. Add pork to the bowl and coat. Transfer the pork to the instant pot and pour over the remaining sauce. Cover and cook on High for 1 hour. Naturally release the pressure. Shred the pork with a fork and mix well to soak up the sauce. Serve.

Pork Chops with Peppers

Cook time: 20 minutes| Serves: 5| Per serving: Calories 407; Carbs 5.4g; Fat 30.8g; Protein 25g

Ingredients:

- Pork chops – 1 lb. cut into bite-sized pieces
- Red bell peppers – 2, sliced
- Chili peppers – 2, chopped
- Small onions – 2, finely chopped
- Bacon slices – 2, chopped
- Butter - 2 tbsps. unsalted
- Beef broth – 1 cup
- Italian seasoning – 2 tsps.
- Salt – ¼ tsp.

Directions:

Rinse the meat, pat dry and sprinkle with 1 tsp. of Italian seasoning. Place in the IP and pour in the broth. Cover and cook 10 minutes on High. Open and remove the meat from the pot along with the broth and press Sauté. Grease the inner pot with the butter and add onion. Sauté for 2 minutes and then add peppers. Sprinkle with salt and remaining Italian seasoning and cook for 2 to 3 minutes. Now add the bacon and stir well. If necessary, add some beef broth, about 2 tbsps. at a time. Finally, add the meat and give it a good stir. Cook for 5 minutes. Serve.

Green Beans with Pork and Potatoes

Cook time: 22 minutes| Serves: 4| Per serving: Calories 180; Carbs 17g; Fat 6g; Protein 15g

Ingredients:

- Lean pork – 1 pound, cubed
- Tomatoes – 3, chopped
- Carrots – 2, peeled and sliced
- Celery – 2 sticks, sliced
- Green beans – 1 pound
- Medium potatoes – 2, peeled and quartered
- White onion – 1, peeled and chopped
- Salt – ½ tsp.
- Ground black pepper - ½ tsp.
- Olive oil – 2 tbsps.

Directions:

Add oil and Press Sauté on the Instant Pot. Add the meat and cook for 5 minutes or until golden brown. Then add the remaining ingredients and mix. Cover and cook 17 minutes on High. Do a quick release and open. Serve.

Coffee Flavored Pork Ribs

Cook time: 40 minutes |Serves: 4| Per serving: Calories 345; Carbs 1.3g; Fat 29.3g; Protein 18.1g

Ingredients:

- Baby back ribs – 1 rack
- Olive oil – 2 tsps.
- Oyster sauce – 3 tbsps.
- Salt – ½ tsp.
- Sugar – 1 tsp.
- Water – 1 cup
- Liquid smoke – ½ cup
- Instant coffee powder – 2 tbsps.

Directions:

Add everything in the pot. Cover and cook 40 minutes on High. Do a natural release and serve.

Pork and Fennel Soup

Cook time: 20 minutes| Serves: 4| Per serving: Calories 162; Carbs 8g; Fat 10g; Protein 14g

Ingredients:

- Fennel bulb – 1, shredded
- Chicken stock – 4 cups

- Yellow onion – 1, chopped
- Pork meat – 1 pound, chopped
- Olive oil – 1 tbsp.
- Salt and pepper to taste
- Tomato sauce – 2 tbsps.
- Parsley – 1 tbsp. chopped

Directions:

Heat oil on Sauté. Add onion and meat and cook for 5 minutes. Add the rest of the ingredients, except for the parsley and cover. Cook on High for 15 minutes. Serve topped with parsley.

Cinnamon Pork Stew
Cook time: 10 minutes| Serves: 4 | Per serving: Calories 231; Carbs 7g; Fat 12g; Protein 9g

Ingredients:

- Pork shoulder – 1 ½ pounds, cubed
- Yellow onion – 1, chopped
- Olive oil – 2 tbsps.
- Cinnamon powder – 1 tsp.
- Garlic – 2 cloves, chopped
- Salt and pepper to taste
- Beef stock – ½ cup
- Canned tomatoes – 12 ounces, chopped
- Basil – 1 tbsp. chopped

Directions:

Heat oil on Sauté. Add meat, onion, garlic and cinnamon and cook for 5 minutes. Add the rest of the ingredients, except for the basil. Cover and cook on Low for 25 minutes. Serve topped with basil.

Sweet Potato and Pork Stew
Cook time: 30 minutes| Serves: 4| Per serving: Calories 200; Carbs 7g; Fat 12g; Protein 14g

Ingredients:

- Yellow onion – 1, chopped
- Olive oil – 1 tbsp.
- Garlic – 2 cloves, minced
- Sweet potatoes – 3, chopped
- Pork stew meat – 1 pound, cubed
- Canned tomatoes – 14 ounces, chopped
- Curry powder – 2 tsps.
- Juice of 2 limes
- Cilantro – 1 tbsp. chopped

Directions:

Heat oil on Sauté. Add onion, garlic and meat. Cook for 5 minutes. Add the remaining ingredients, except the cilantro. Cover and cook for 25 minutes on High. Serve topped with cilantro.

Sage Pork Stew

Cook time: 30 minutes| Serves: 4| Per serving: Calories 220; Carbs 7g; Fat 12g; Protein 16g

Ingredients:

- Yellow onion – 1, chopped
- Pork stew meat – 2 pounds, cubed
- Olive oil – 2 tbsps.
- Carrots – 3, chopped
- Beef stock – 1 cup
- Garlic – 2 cloves, minced
- Salt and pepper to taste
- Sage – 1 tbsp. chopped for garnishing

Directions:

Heat oil on sauté. Add meat, onion, and garlic and cook for 5 minutes. Add rest of the ingredients and cover. Cook on Low for 25 minutes. Serve with sage sprinkled on top.

Pork Bites

Cook time: 30 minutes| Serves: 4| Per serving: Calories 242; Carbs 6g; Fat 12g; Protein 14g

Ingredients:

- Pork roast – 1 pound, cubed and browned
- Italian seasoning – 1 tbsp.
- Beef stock – 1 cup
- Water – 2 tbsps.
- Sweet paprika – 1 tbsp.
- Tomato sauce – 2 tbsps.
- Rosemary – 1 tbsp. chopped

Directions:

Add everything in the pot, except the rosemary. Mix and cover. Cook on High for 30 minutes. Serve sprinkle with rosemary.

Pork Chops with Apples

Cook time: 25 minutes |Serves: 4| Per serving: Calories 210; Carbs 8g; Fat 5g; Protein 12g

Ingredients:

- Pork chops – 4
- Oil – 2 tbsps.
- Garlic – 1 clove, minced
- Lemon juice – 2 tbsps.
- Green apples – 2, cored and cubed

- Yellow onion – 1, chopped
- Beef stock – ½ cup
- Salt and pepper to taste
- Parsley – 1 tbsp. chopped

Directions:

Heat oil on Sauté. Add onion and garlic and sauté for 2 minutes. Add pork chops and cook for 3 minutes. Add the rest of the ingredients, expect for the parsley. Cover and cook for 20 minutes on High. Serve.

Tomato Pork Chops
Cook time: 25 minutes| Serves: 4| Per serving: Calories 233; Carbs 7g; Fat 9g ; Protein 14g

Ingredients:

- Pork chops – 4
- Veggie stock – 1 cup
- Tomato puree – ¼ cup
- Sweet paprika – 4 tsps.
- Salt and pepper to taste

Directions:

Combine everything in the pot and cover. Cook on High for 25 minutes. Serve.

Sesame Pork Chops
Cook time: 25 minutes| Serves: 4| Per serving: Calories 236; Carbs 7g; Fat 12g; Protein 15g

Ingredients:

- Pork chops – 4
- Sesame seeds – 2 tsps.
- Oil – 1 tbsp.
- Chili powder – 1 tsp.
- Sweet paprika – 1 tsp.
- Tomato sauce – 1 cup
- Chives – 1 tbsp. chopped

Directions:

Heat oil on Sauté. Add pork chops and brown for 5 minutes. Add the rest of the ingredients, except the sesame seeds. Cover and cook on High for 20 minutes. Serve.

Pork Chops and Cauliflower Rice
Cook time: 25 minutes| Serves: 4| Per serving: Calories 244; Carbs 5 g; Fat 12g; Protein 16g

Ingredients:

- Beef stock – 2 cups
- Peppercorns – 1 tbsp. crushed

- Cauliflower rice - 1 cup
- Garlic – 4 cloves, minced
- Pork chops – 4
- Red onion – 1, chopped
- Olive oil – 2 tbsps.
- Salt and pepper to taste

Directions:

Heat oil on Sauté. Add onion and garlic and Sauté for 2 minutes. Add meat and brown for 3 minutes. Add the rest of the ingredients and cover. Cook on High for 20 minutes. Serve.

Rosemary Pork and Green Beans

Cook time: 25 minutes| Serves: 4| Per serving: Calories 254; Carbs 6g; Fat 14g; Protein 17g

Ingredients:

- Pork loin – 1 ½ pounds, sliced
- Green beans – 1 pound, trimmed
- Veggie stock – 1 ½ cup
- Garlic – 3 cloves, minced
- Rosemary – 1 bunch, chopped
- Salt and pepper to taste
- Yellow onion – 1, chopped

Directions:

Combine everything in the pot. Cover and cook on High for 25 minutes. Serve.

Mustard Pork Ribs

Cook time: 30 minutes| Serves: 4| Per serving: Calories 263; Carbs 6g; Fat 14g; Protein 20g

Ingredients:

- Pork ribs – 2 pounds
- Salt and pepper to taste
- Smoked paprika – 1 tbsp.
- Dijon mustard – 2 tbsps.
- Sage – 1 tbsp. chopped
- Olive oil – 1 tbsp.
- Beef stock – 1 ½ cups
- Cilantro – 1 tbsp. chopped

Directions:

Heat oil on Sauté. Add the ribs and the rest of the ingredients, except for the stock and cilantro. Cook for 5 minutes. Add stock and cover. Cook on High for 25 minutes. Serve topped with parsley.

Oregano and Spring Onion Pork

Cook time: 35 minutes |Serves: 4 | Per serving: Calories 253; Carbs 6g; Fat 14g; Protein 17g

Ingredients:

- Green onions – 4, chopped
- Pork chops – 4
- Oil – 2 tsps.
- Garlic – 3 cloves, minced
- Oregano – 1 tbsp. chopped
- Beef stock – 1 ½ cups
- Tomato sauce – 2 tbsps.
- Cilantro – 1 tbsp. chopped

Directions:

Heat oil on Sauté. Add onions and garlic and cook for 2 minutes. Add meat and brown for 3 minutes. Add the rest of the ingredients and cover. Cook on High for 30 minutes. Serve.

Pork Chops and Bell Peppers

Cook time: 35 minutes |Serves: 4| Per serving: Calories 273; Carbs 5g; Fat 13g; Protein 15g

Ingredients:

- Oil – 2 tbsps.
- Pork chops – 4
- Salt and pepper to taste
- Bell peppers – 2, chopped
- Garlic – 3 cloves, chopped
- Red onion – 1, chopped
- Beef stock - 2 cups
- Parsley – 1 tbsp. chopped

Directions:

Heat oil on Sauté. Add pork and brown for 2 minutes. Add onion and garlic and brown for 3 minutes more. Add all the other ingredients, except the parsley. Cover and cook on High for 30 minutes. Sprinkle with parsley and serve.

Pork, Corn and Green Beans

Cook time: 35 minutes| Serves: 4| Per serving: Calories 264; Carbs 8g; Fat 14g; Protein 12g

Ingredients:

- Pork shoulder – 2 pounds, boneless and cubed
- Garlic – 2 cloves, minced
- Salt and pepper to taste
- Corn – 1 cup
- Green beans – 1 cup trimmed and halved
- Beef stock – 1 cup

- Cumin – 1 tsp. ground

Directions:

Combine everything in the pot. Cover and cook on High for 35 minutes. Open and serve.

Pork Shoulder and Celery

Cook time: 30 minutes |Serves: 4 | Per serving: Calories 234; Carbs 7g; Fat 11g; Protein 15g

Ingredients:

- Pork shoulder – 2 pounds, boneless and cubed
- Oil – 2 tbsps.
- Salt and pepper to taste
- Chili powder – 2 tbsps.
- Celery – 2 stalks, chopped
- Garlic – 4 cloves, minced
- Beef stock – 1 ½ cups
- Sage – 1 tbsp. chopped

Directions:

Heat oil on Sauté. Add garlic and cook for 2 minutes. Add the meat and cook for 3 minutes more. Add the rest of the ingredients and cover. Cook on High for 25 minutes. Serve.

Pork, Spinach and Dill

Cook time: 25 minutes| Serves: 4| Per serving: Calories 277; Carbs 7g; Fat 14g; Protein 17g

Ingredients:

- Pork stew meat – 1 ½ pounds, cubed
- Oil – 2 tbsps.
- Yellow onion – ½ cup, chopped
- Baby spinach – 2 cups
- Tomatoes – 2, cubed
- Beef stock – 1 ½ cups
- Dill – 1 tbsp. chopped

Directions:

Heat oil on Sauté. Add onion and meat and cook for 3 minutes. Add the rest of the ingredients and cover. Cook on High for 20 minutes. Serve.

Pork and Ginger Broccoli

Cook time: 30 minutes |Serves: 4 | Per serving: Calories 269; Carbs 5g; Fat 12g; Protein 16g

Ingredients:

- Pork stew meat – 1 ½ pounds, cubed
- Oil – 1 tbsp.
- Broccoli florets – 2 cups

- Ginger – 1 tbsp. grated
- Parmesan – ¾ cup, grated
- Salt and pepper to taste
- Tomato puree – ¼ cup
- Beef stock – 1 ½ cups
- Basil – 1 tbsp. chopped

Directions:

Heat oil on Sauté. Add meat and cook for 5 minutes. Add the rest of the ingredients, except the basil and parmesan. Cover and cook on High for 25 minutes. Open and sprinkle with parmesan and basil. Cover and leave aside for 5 minutes. Serve.

Tarragon Pork Mix
Cook time: 30 minutes |Serves: 4 | Per serving: Calories 263; Carbs 6g; Fat 12g; Protein 13g

Ingredients:

- Red onion – 1, chopped
- Tarragon – 1 tbsp. chopped
- Oregano – ½ tsp. dried
- Salt and pepper to taste
- Pork stew meat - 1 ½ pounds, cubed
- Olive oil – 1 tbsp.
- Tomato puree – 1 cup

Directions:

Heat oil on Sauté. Add meat and onion and cook for 5 minutes. Add the rest of the ingredients and cover. Cook on High for 25 minutes. Open and serve.

Chapter 9 Beef and Lamb Recipes

Spicy Lamb

Cook time: 30 minutes| Serves: 6| Per serving: Calories 350; Carbs 1.9 g; Fat 17.4g; Protein 43.3g

Ingredients:

- Boneless leg of lamb – 2 lbs. cut into bite-sized pieces
- Heavy cream – ¼ cup
- Ghee – 2 tbsps.
- Cherry tomatoes – 2 cups, chopped
- Vegetable stock – 3 cups
- Salt – 1 tsp.
- Coriander powder – 1 tbsp.
- Ginger powder – 1 tsp.
- Cumin powder – 1 tsp.
- Chili powder – 2 tbsps.
- Garam masala – 1 tsp.
- Garlic powder – ½ tsp.
- Fennel seeds – 2 tsps.
- Cumin seeds – 1 ½ tsp.
- Whole cloves – 3
- Cinnamon stick – 1
- Bay leaves – 3

Directions:

Place the chopped lamb pieces in a deep bowl and add heavy cream and garam masala. Mix and tightly wrap with aluminum foil. Refrigerate overnight. Grease the inner pot with ghee and press Sauté. Add fennel seeds, cumin seeds, cloves, cinnamon, cardamom, and bay leaves. Cook and stir for 1 to 2 minutes. Now add the remaining spices and stir well. Cook for another minute. Add the marinated meat. Pour in the stock and add cherry tomatoes. Stir well and close. Cook 25 minutes on High. Serve.

Lamb Curry with Zucchini

Cook time: 27 minutes |Serves: 4| Per serving: Calories 338; Carbs 7.5g; Fat 21g; Protein 23g

Ingredients:

- Ghee – 1 tbsp.
- Minced garlic – 2 tsps.
- Lamb – 1 pound, cut into cubes
- Grated ginger – 1 tsp.
- Diced tomatoes – 1 cup
- Coconut milk – ½ cup
- Zucchini – 1, diced
- Onion – 1, diced

- Carrot – 1, thinly sliced
- Curry powder – 1 ½ tbsps.

Directions:

In a bowl, place the coconut milk, lamb, ginger, and garlic. Cover and place in the fridge for 3 hours. Now add the lamb and the juices to the pot. Add the ghee, tomatoes, onion, and carrot. Close and cook for 20 minutes on High. Do a natural pressure release. Stir in the zucchini and cook on Sauté for 5 to 6 minutes. Serve.

Cheesy Cajun Beef
Cook time: 17 minutes |Serves: 4| Per serving: Calories 400; Carbs 4g; Fat 16g; Protein 33g

Ingredients:

- Cajun seasoning – 1 tbsp.
- Mexican cheese blend – 12 ounces
- Beef broth – 1 cup
- Ground beef – 1 pound
- Tomato paste – 2 tbsps.
- Olive oil – 1 tbsp.

Directions:

Press Sauté and heat the oil. Add beef and cook until browned. Stir in the tomato paste and seasoning. Pour the broth over and close the lid. Cook on High for 7 minutes. Stir in the cheese and cook on High for 5 more minutes. Do a quick pressure release. Serve.

Balsamic Fried Beef Roast
Cook time: 27 minutes| Serves: 8| Per serving: Calories 464; Carbs 2.5g; Fat 36.1g; Protein 30.2g

Ingredients:

- Beef chuck roast – 2 lbs. cut into bite-sized pieces
- Shallots – ½ cup, chopped
- Garlic – 3 cloves, crushed
- Balsamic vinegar – ¼ cup
- Heavy cream – ½ cup
- Olive oil – 1 tbsp.
- Salt – 1 tsp.
- Dried oregano – 1 tsp. ground
- Black pepper – 1 tsp. ground
- Dried parsley – 1 tbsp. finely chopped
- Dried marjoram – ¼ tsp. ground

Directions:

Rub the beef pieces with salt and pepper and set aside. Grease the instant pot with oil. Add shallots and garlic. Stir-fry for 2 to 3 minutes, stirring constantly. Add the meat and cook for 10 minutes. Pour in the balsamic vinegar and heavy cream. Sprinkle with the remaining spices and mix. Bring to a boil and cook until sauce thickens, about 10 to 15 minutes. Transfer to a serving dish. Drizzle with lemon juice and serve.

Beef Stroganoff

Cook time: 20 minutes |Serves: 4| Per serving: Calories 260; Carbs 4.8g; Fat 14g; Protein 26.5g

Ingredients:

- Small onion – 1, diced
- Garlic – 2 cloves, crushed
- Bacon – 2 rashers, diced
- Beef Sirloin Steak – 1 lbs. (cut into ½ inch strips)
- Smoked paprika – 1 tsp.
- Tomato paste – 3 tbsps.
- Beef broth – 1 cup
- Mushrooms – ½ lbs. quartered
- Sour cream – ½ cup

Directions:

Except for the sour cream, place all ingredients in the pot and stir to combine. Cover and cook for 20 minutes on high. Naturally release the pressure, then stir in the sour cream. Serve warm.

Classic Beef Stew

Cook time: 15 minutes |Serves: 5| Per serving: Calories 208; Carbs 4.7g; Fat 6.4g; Protein 31.2g

Ingredients:

- Avocado oil - 2 tbsps.
- Beef stew meat – 1 pound, cubed
- Garlic – 1 clove, minced
- Bone broth – 3 cups
- Wild mushrooms – 2 ounces
- Carrots – 2
- Bay leaf – 1
- Dried parsley – ½ tsp.
- Salt – ½ tsp.
- Ground black pepper – ½ tsp.

Directions:

Press Sauté, add oil and heat. Add beef and cook until browned. Stirring occasionally. Add garlic and cook for 1 minute more. Add the salt, black pepper, parsley, bay leaf, carrots, mushrooms, and bone broth. Close and cook 15 minutes on High. Do a natural release. Open, remove bay leaf and serve.

Traditional Goulash

Cook time: 18 minutes| Serves: 5| Per serving: Calories 255; Carbs 7.5g; Fat 12.3g; Protein 29g

Ingredients:

- Coconut oil – 2 tbsps.
- Beef stew meat – 1 pound, cubed
- Avocado oil – 2 tbsps.
- Paprika – 2 tbsps.
- Minced garlic – 1 tsp.
- Ground cumin – ½ tsp.
- Coriander – ½ tsp.
- Onion – ½, chopped
- Ground cayenne pepper – ½ tsp.
- Salt – ½ tsp.
- Ground black pepper – ½ tsp.
- Diced tomatoes – 1 (14-ounce) can
- Water – 4 cups

Directions:

Melt the coconut oil on Sauté in the Instant Pot. Brown the beef and set aside. Clean the inner pot and add avocado oil. Sauté tomatoes, black pepper, salt, cayenne pepper, onion, coriander, cumin, garlic, and paprika for 3 minutes. Add water and stir. Close and cook 18 minutes on High. Do a natural release. Open and serve.

Mushroom Burgers

Cook time: 20 minutes| Serves: 2| Per serving: Calories 510; Carbs 7.6g; Fat 33.5g; Protein 40.5g

Ingredients:

- Beef – 1 pound, ground
- Cayenne pepper – ½ tsp. ground
- Oregano – ½ tsp. dried
- Ground black pepper – ½ tsp.
- Salt – ½ tsp.
- Portobello mushroom caps – 4
- Lettuce – 1 cup, shredded
- Tomatoes – 1 cup, diced
- Dijon mustard – 1 tsp.
- Small onion – ¼, thinly sliced
- Full-fat cheddar cheese – ½ cup shredded

Directions:

Preheat the oven to 350F. Lightly grease a baking sheet and place the mushroom caps on it. Add ½ cup water to the Instant Pot. Insert the trivet. Mix beef, salt, black pepper, oregano, and cayenne pepper in a bowl. Make 2 patties and place the patties on top of the trivet. Close and cook 20 minutes on High. Meanwhile, Bake the mushroom caps in the oven, 5 minutes per side. Do a natural pressure release. Open the lid and remove the meat. Arrange the burgers with mushroom caps, patties, and remaining ingredients. Serve.

Steak and Cauliflower Rice
Cook time: 20 minutes| Serves: 4|Per serving: Calories 418; Carbs 8.5 g; Fat 22.1g; Protein 54.4g

Ingredients:

- Ribeye steak – 1
- Fresh paprika – ½ tsp.
- Ground turmeric – ½ tsp.
- Dried parsley – ½ tsp.
- Ground cumin – ½ tsp.
- Ground black pepper – ½ tsp.
- Salt – ½ tsp.
- Cauliflower head – 1, chopped
- Butter – 2 tbsps. softened
- Avocado – 1, mashed

Directions:

Add 1-cup of water into the Instant Pot and place in the trivet. In a bowl, mix salt, black pepper, cumin, parsley, turmeric, and paprika. Coat the steak with this mixture. Place the coated steak onto a greased dish. Place the cauliflower beside the steak. Place the dish on top of the trivet and cover loosely with foil. Close and cook for 20 minutes on High. Do a natural release. Remove the dish and add butter to the steak. Serve with avocado.

Balsamic Beef
Cook time: 22 minutes| Serves: 4| Per serving: Calories 323; Carbs 3.1g; Fat 15.6g; Protein 39.5g

Ingredients:

- Chunk roast – 1 pound
- Garlic – 2 cloves, minced
- Bone broth – 1 cup
- Ground rosemary – ½ tsp.
- Ground black pepper – ½ tsp.
- Salt – ½ tsp.
- Ground thyme – ½ tsp.
- Crushed red pepper – ½ tsp.
- Balsamic vinegar – ¼ cup

- Butter – 4 tbsps. softened
- Broccoli – 1 cup, chopped
- Water – ½ cup

Directions:

Add the water and chuck roast to the pot. Close and cook for 20 minutes on High. Combine 2 tbsps. butter, vinegar, red pepper, thyme, salt, black pepper, rosemary, bone broth, and garlic in a bowl. Mix well. Do a natural release when cooked. Open the pot and remove the dish. Press Sauté and add 2 tbsps. butter and broccoli. Cook broccoli until cooked. Remove broccoli. Serve the beef with broccoli, and sauce.

Lamb with Tomatoes

Cook time: 26 minutes| Serves: 4| Per serving: Calories 338; Carbs 7.5g; Fat 21g; Protein 23g

Ingredients:

- Ghee – 1 tbsp.
- Minced garlic – 2 tsps.
- Lamb – 1 pound, cut into cubes
- Grated ginger – 1 tsp.
- Diced tomatoes – 1 cup
- Coconut milk – ½ cup
- Zucchini – 1, diced
- Onion – 1, diced
- Carrot – 1, thinly sliced
- Curry powder – 1 ½ tbsp.

Directions:

In a bowl, place the coconut milk, lamb, ginger, and garlic. Cover and place in the fridge for 3 hours. Now add the lamb and the juices to the Instant Pot. Add the ghee, tomatoes, onion, and carrot. Close and cook for 20 minutes on High. Do a natural pressure release. Stir in the zucchini and cook on Sauté for 5 to 6 minutes. Serve.

Picadillo

Cook time: 20 minutes| Serves: 6| Per serving: Calories 207; Carbs 4g; Fat 8.5g; Protein 25g

Ingredients:

- Olive oil – 1 tbsp.
- Lean ground beef – 1 ½ lbs.
- Salt – 1 tsp.
- Ground black pepper – 1 tsp.
- Onion – 3 ½ oz. diced
- Garlic – 2 cloves, minced

- Tomato – 6 oz. diced
- Coriander leaves – 2 tbsps. chopped
- Olives – 6, stuffed with pepper
- Capers – 6
- Cumin – 1 tsp.
- Red bell pepper – ½ diced
- Tomato sauce – 4 oz.
- Bay leaf – 1
- Water – 5 tbsps.

Directions:

Press Sauté and add 1 tbsp. oil in the Instant Pot. Add the beef and stir-fry until brown, about 3 to 4 minutes. Add coriander leaves, salt, pepper, chopped tomato, garlic, and onion. Stir-fry for 1 minute. Add the water, bay leaf, tomato sauce, bell pepper, cumin, capers, and olives. Stir to combine. Cover and cook on High for 15 minutes. Do a natural release and serve.

Grilled Beef Tenderloin
Cook time: 25 minutes| Serves: 6| Per serving: Calories 562; Carbs 2.4g; Fat 28.3g; Protein 69.7g

Ingredients:

- Beef tenderloin – 2 lbs. cut into bite-sized pieces
- Garlic – 4 cloves, finely chopped
- Beef broth – 3 cups
- Olive oil – 1 tbsp.
- Butter – 1 tbsp.
- Onion powder – 1 tsp.
- Dried oregano – 1 tsp. ground
- Dried rosemary – 1 tsp. ground
- Sea salt – 1 tsp.
- Black pepper – 1 tsp. ground
- Chives and thyme for garnish

Directions:

Place the chopped meat in a bowl. Add all the spices. Rub well and set aside. Grease the insert with olive oil and press Sauté. Add garlic and chopped tenderloin, cook for 5 minutes. Add beef broth and cover the lid. Cook on High for 20 minutes. Do a quick release and open. Garnish with chives and thyme and serve.

Beef Stew
Cook time: 25 minutes | Serves: 8| Per serving: Calories 268; Carbs 21g; Fat 8.1g; Protein 29g

Ingredients:

- Stew beef – 1 ½ pound, cut into bite-sized pieces

- Red pepper – 1, chopped
- Small potatoes – 4, cubed
- Zucchini – 2, sliced
- Mushrooms – 10 ounces, chopped
- Salt – ½ tsp.
- Ground black pepper – 1 tsp.
- Dried sage – ½ tsp.
- Dried thyme – 1 tsp.
- Olive oil – 1 tbsp.
- Red wine – 1 ½ cup
- Water – 1 ½ cup

Directions:

Press Sauté and add oil to the Instant Pot. Add beef and cook for 5 minutes. Add remaining ingredients and mix. Cover. Cook on High for 20 minutes. Open and serve.

Rosemary Lamb
Cook time: 50 minutes| Serves: 8| Per serving: Calories 318; Carbs 3g; Fat 17g; Protein 37g

Ingredients:

- Onions – 2, chopped
- Rosemary – 2 sprigs
- Beef broth – 3 cups, low-sodium
- Lamb shanks – 2, about 1 pound each
- Bay leaves – 2
- Olive oil – 3 tbsps.
- Salt to taste

Directions:

Add oil in the Instant Pot and press Sauté. Add meat and cook for 5 minutes or until browned. Set aside. Add onions. Cook for 3 to 4 minutes or until translucent. Add meat and pour in the broth. Add remaining ingredients and cover. Cook on High for 40 minutes. Then do a quick release. Open and remove the rosemary and bay leaves. Serve.

Lamb Stew with Bacon
Cook time: 28 minutes |Serves: 6| Per serving: Calories 453; Carbs 3.8g; Fat 23.6g; Protein 52.5g

Ingredients:

- Lamb leg – 2 pounds, chopped
- Olive oil – 2 tbsps.
- Garlic – 8 cloves
- Bacon – 6 slices

- Beef broth – 3 cups
- Onion – 1, chopped
- Black pepper – ¼ tsp.
- Dried rosemary – 1 tsp.
- Salt – ½ tsp.

Directions:

Press Sauté on the Instant Pot and add oil. Add onions and bacon and stir-fry for 3 minutes. Meanwhile, make 8 incisions into the meat and place a garlic clove in each. Rub with spices and transfer to the pot. Pour in broth and the remaining ingredients, cover. Cook 25 minutes on High. Open and serve.

Greek Lamb Stew
Cook time: 30 minutes | Serves: 4| Per serving: Calories 242; Carbs 9g; Fat 12g; Protein 15g

Ingredients:

- Lamb shoulder – 2 pounds, cubed
- Garlic – 1 tbsp. minced
- Canned tomatoes – 14 ounces, chopped
- Yellow onion – 2, chopped
- Olive oil – 1 tbsp.
- Oregano – 1 tsp. dried
- Basil – 1 tsp. dried
- Salt and pepper to taste
- Parsley – ½ cup, chopped

Directions:

Heat oil on Sauté. Add onion, garlic and meat and cook for 5 minutes. Add the rest of the ingredients except the parsley. Cover and cook on High for 25 minutes. Serve garnished with parsley.

Lamb Ribs
Cook time: 25 minutes| Serves: 4| Per serving: Calories 263; Carbs 7g; Fat 12g; Protein 12g

Ingredients:

- Lamb ribs – 4
- Garlic – 4 cloves, minced
- Sage – 1 tbsp. chopped
- Veggie stock – 1 ½ cups
- Olive oil – 2 tbsps.
- Salt and pepper to taste
- Tomatoes – 2, cubed

Directions:

Heat oil on Sauté. Add lamb, garlic, sage, salt, and pepper and brown for 5 minutes. Add the stock and tomatoes and cover. Cook on High for 20 minutes. Serve.

Lamb Chops

Cook time: 40 minutes| Serves: 4| Per serving: Calories 238; Carbs 5g; Fat 10g; Protein 15g

Ingredients:

- Lamb chops – 4
- Veggie stock – 1 cup
- Dill – 1 tsp. dried
- Garlic powder – 1 tsp.
- Chili flakes – 1 tsp. crushed
- Chives – 1 tbsp. chopped
- Oil – 1 tbsp.
- Salt and pepper to taste

Directions:

Heat oil on Sauté. Add lamb chops and brown for 2 minutes on each side. Add the rest of the ingredient and cover. Cook on Low for 35 minutes. Serve.

Beef and Lamb Mix

Cook time: 35 minutes| Serves: 4| Per serving: Calories 272; Carbs 7g; Fat 14g; Protein 17g

Ingredients:

- Beef stew meat – 1 pound, cubed
- Lamb shoulder – 1 pound, cubed
- Garlic – 4 cloves, minced
- Red bell peppers – 2, cut into strips
- Oil – 1 tbsp.
- Celery stalks – 2, chopped
- Carrots – 2, chopped
- Thyme – ¼ tsp. dried
- Salt and pepper to taste
- Oregano – 1 tbsp. chopped
- Beef stock – 1 ½ cups

Directions:

Heat oil on Sauté. Add the garlic and the meat and brown for 5 minutes. Add the rest of the ingredients and cover. Cook on High for 30 minutes. Open and serve.

Chapter 10 Fish and Seafood Recipes

Salmon with Vegetables
Cook time: 5 minutes| Serves: 4| Per serving: Calories 188; Carbs 7g; Fat 8.9g; Protein 17.7g

Ingredients:

- Fresh parsley – a ½ bunch, plus more for garnish
- Fresh tarragon – 2 to 3 sprigs
- Wild salmon fillets – 1 ½ pounds
- Olive oil – 1 tbsp.
- Sea salt and black pepper to taste
- Lemon – 1, sliced
- Medium zucchinis – 2, julienned
- Medium bell pepper – 2, seeded and julienned
- Medium carrots – 2, julienned

Directions:

Add tarragon, parsley and ¾ cup water into the Instant Pot. Place the steamer rack in the IP. Drizzle the salmon with olive oil and season with salt and pepper. Place the salmon on the rack (skin-side down). Top with lemon slices. Close the lid and press Steam. Steam for 3 minutes. Do a quick release and remove the rack with the salmon. Keep the salmon warm. Keep the liquid and discard the herbs. Add the carrots, peppers, and zucchinis to the IP and close the lid. Press Sauté and cook for 2 to 3 minutes. When the vegetables are tender, remove and season with salt and pepper. Serve.

Simple Crab Legs
Cook time: 3 minutes| Serves: 5| Per serving: Calories 152; Carbs 0g; Fat 23g; Protein 16g

Ingredients:

- Crab legs – 2 pounds, thawed
- Water – 1 cup for the pot

Directions:

Add 1-cup water into the IP and insert trivet. Place the crab legs on top of the trivet. Press Manual and cook on High for 3 minutes. Do a quick release. Serve crab legs with your favorite sauce.

Crab Bisque
Cook time: 3 minutes| Serves: 4| Per serving: Calories 415; Carbs 8g; Fat 35.1g ; Protein 13g

Ingredients:

- Butter – 4 tbsps.
- Bone broth – 3 cups
- Full-fat cream cheese – 8 ounces, softened

- Celery – 2 stalks, chopped
- Crab meat – 1 pound, thawed
- Old Bay Seasoning – 1 tsp.
- Cayenne pepper – ½ tsp. ground
- Ground black pepper – ½ tsp.
- Salt – ½ tsp.
- Bell peppers – ¼ cup, chopped
- Heavy whipping cream – ¼ cup
- Small onion – ¼, sliced
- Crushed tomatoes – 1 (14-ounce) can

Directions:

Melt the butter on Sauté in the Instant Pot. Pour in the bone broth and add tomatoes, onion, whipping cream, bell pepper, salt, pepper, cayenne pepper, Old Bay, crab, celery, and cream cheese. Mix. Close the lid and cook on Manual for 3 minutes on Low. Do a quick release and open. Blend with a hand mixer. Serve.

Salmon with Broccoli

Cook time: 4 minutes |Serves: 4 | Per serving: Calories 119; Carbs 4g; Fat 5g; Protein 16g

Ingredients:

- Salmon fillets – 4
- Water – 1 ½ cups
- Broccoli fillets – 10 ounces
- Garlic powder – 1 tsp.
- Salt and pepper to taste

Directions:

Season the salmon with garlic powder, salt, and pepper. Pour the water into the Instant Pot. Place the salmon in the steaming basket and add the broccoli around the fish. Close the lid and cook on High for 4 minutes. Quick release and serve.

Cajun Shrimp with Asparagus

Cook time: 2 minutes| Serves: 4 | Per serving: Calories 330; Carbs 7g; Fat 7g; Protein 45g

Ingredients:

- Cajun seasoning – 1 tbsp.
- Shrimp – 1 pound, peeled and deveined
- Asparagus – 1 bunch, trimmed
- Olive oil – 1 tsp.
- Salt and pepper to taste

Directions:

Pour the water into the IP. Arrange the asparagus in a single layer on the IP's rack. Top with the shrimp. Drizzle with oil and season with Cajun, salt and pepper. Close the lid and cook on Steam for 2 minutes. Do a quick pressure release. Serve.

Dijon Halibut
Cook time: 3 minutes| Serves: 4| Per serving: Calories 190; Carbs 0.1g; Fat 2g; Protein 40g

Ingredients:

- Dijon mustard – 1 ½ tbsps.
- Halibut fillets – 4
- Water – 1 ½ cups

Directions:

Pour the water into the IP. Brush the halibut with Dijon and place in the steaming basket. Lower the basket and close the lid. Set the IP to Manual. Cook on High for 3 minutes. Do a quick pressure release. Serve.

Sockeye Salmon
Cook time: 4 minutes |Serves: 4| Per serving: Calories 195; Carbs 1g; Fat 10g; Protein 24g

Ingredients:

- Dijon mustard – 1 tsp.
- Garlic powder – 1 tsp.
- Onion powder – ¼ tsp.
- Garlic – 1 clove, minced
- Salmon fillets – 4 (2 to 3 ounce each)
- Lemon juice – 1 tbsp.
- Salt and pepper to taste
- Water – 1 ½ cups

Directions:

Combine the lemon juice, minced garlic, garlic powder, onion powder, and mustard in a small bowl. Brush the mixture over the salmon. Pour the water into the IP and lower the rack. Arrange the salmon on the rack and close the lid. Cook on High for 4 minutes. Do a quick pressure release. Serve.

Shrimp Zoodles
Cook time: 5 minutes| Serves: 4 | Per serving: Calories 300; Carbs 3g; Fat 20g; Protein 30g

Ingredients:

- Zoodles – 4 cups
- Ghee – 2 tbsp.

- Veggie stock – 1 cup
- Olive oil – 2 tbsps.
- Minced garlic – 3 tsps.
- Shrimp – 1 pound, peeled and deveined
- Juice of ½ lemon
- Chopped basil – 1 tbsp.
- Paprika – ½ tsp.

Directions:

Melt the ghee along with olive oil in the Instant Pot on Sauté. Add garlic and cook for 1 minute. Add shrimp and lemon juice. Cook for 1 minute. Add stock, paprika, and zoodles. Cook on High for 3 minutes. Serve topped with basil. Enjoy.

Steamed Tuna Steaks
Cook time: 4 minutes| Serves: 4| Per serving: Calories 190; Carbs 1g ; Fat 3g; Protein 39.5g

Ingredients:

- Tuna steaks – 4 (4-ounce each)
- Capers – 2 tbsps.
- Lemon pepper seasoning – 1 tbsp.
- Lemon juice – 2 tbsps.
- Water – 1 cup

Directions:

Pour water in the Instant Pot. Then insert a steamer basket. Season tuna with lemon pepper seasoning and sprinkle with capers. Place into the steamer basket and drizzle with lemon juice. Cover the pot and cook on Steam for 4 minutes on High. Do a natural release and open. Serve.

Shrimp with Tomatoes and Feta
Cook time: 2 minutes | Serves: 6 | Per serving: Calories 211; Carbs 6g; Fat 11g; Protein 19g

Ingredients:

- Frozen shrimp - 1 pound, shelled
- Sliced black olives – ½ cup
- Chopped white onion – 1 ½ cups
- Tomatoes – 14.5 ounces
- Minced garlic – 1 tbsp.
- Salt – 1 tsp.
- Red pepper flakes – ½ tsp.
- Dried oregano – 1 tsp.
- Olive oil – 2 tbsps.
- Feta cheese – 1 cup, crumbled

- Chopped parsley – ¼ cup

Directions:

Heat the oil on Sauté in the Instant Pot. Add garlic and red pepper. Cook for 1 minute. Add onion and tomatoes and season with salt and oregano. Add shrimps, mix, and cover. Cook on Low for 1 minute. Do a natural release and open. Stir shrimps. Sprinkle with olives, cheese, and parsley. Serve.

Clam Chowder II

Cook time: 12 minutes| Serves: 6| Per serving: Calories 252; Carbs 25g; Fat 11g; Protein 12g

Ingredients:

- Bacon – 4 strips, chopped
- Chopped clams – 6.5 ounces
- Large carrots – 3, chopped
- Diced turnip – ¾ cup
- Radishes – 10 medium, trimmed, peeled and quartered
- Red bell pepper – 1, chopped
- Fresh leeks – ¾ cup, diced
- Celery – 3 stalks, diced
- Diced tomatoes – 28 ounces
- Minced garlic – 2 tsps.
- Sea salt – 1 tsp.
- Dried oregano – 1 tbsp.
- Ground thyme – 1 ½ tsps.
- Sambal oiled paste – 1 tsp. (or any chili paste)
- Clam juice – 16 ounces
- Tomato paste – 1 ½ tbsps.
- Bay leaves – 2
- Chopped parsley – 3 tbsps.

Directions:

Cook the bacon on Sauté in the Instant Pot for 2 minutes or until beginning to brown. Remove the bacon and leave 2 tbsps. bacon grease in the pot. Add carrots, bell pepper, and leeks and cook on sauté for 5 minutes. Add the remaining ingredients except for clams and parsley and stir to mix. Cover and cook for 5 minutes on High. Then do a natural release. Add clams and parsley. Stir and serve with crumbled bacon.

Salmon with Green Beans
Cook time: 5 minutes| Serves: 4| Per serving: Calories 303; Carbs 9.3g Fat 14.2g; Protein 36.9g

Ingredients:

- Lemon juice – ¼ cup
- Water – ¾ cup
- Salmon fillets – 4
- Fresh dill – 1 tbsp.
- Salt and pepper to taste
- Lemon slices – 4
- Green beans – 4 cups
- Olive oil – 1 tbsp.

Directions:

Pour the lemon juice and water into the Instant Pot. Add a steamer basket. Place the salmon fillets and green beans on top of the steamer. Sprinkle the dill on top of the salmon and season the salmon and green beans with salt and pepper. Top the fish and green beans with lemon slices. Cover the pot. Then cook on High for 5 minutes. Do a quick release and serve.

Sea Bass with Vegetables
Cook time: 17 minutes| Serves: 4 | Per serving: Calories 235; Carbs 7.5g; Fat 9.3g; Protein 25.3g

Ingredients:

- Olive oil – 4 tsps. divided
- Sea bass fillets – 4
- Onion – 1, diced
- White wine – ½ cup
- Black olives – ½ cup, pitted and chopped
- Capers – 2 tbsps.
- Canned diced tomatoes with juice – 1 cup
- Red pepper – ¼ tsp. crushed
- Baby spinach – 2 cups
- Salt and pepper to taste

Directions:

Press Sauté and add half the oil in the Instant Pot. Add the fish and cook for 5 minutes and remove to a platter. Add the remaining oil and add onion in the Instant Pot. Sauté for 2 minutes. Add the wine and simmer for 2 minutes. Add the capers, olives, tomatoes, and crushed red pepper. Cook for 3 minutes. Stir in the spinach and cook for 5 minutes. Pour the sauce over the fish and serve.

Fish Bowls

Cook time: 10 minutes| Serves: 4| Per serving: Calories 132; Carbs 5 g; Fat 9g; Protein 11g

Ingredients:

- White fish fillets – 1 pound, boneless, skinless and cubed
- Black olives – 1 cup, pitted and chopped
- Cherry tomatoes – 1 pound, halved
- Garlic – 2 cloves, minced
- Oil - 1 tbsp.
- Salt and pepper to taste
- Oregano – 1 tbsp. chopped
- Parsley - 1 tbsp. chopped

Directions:

Heat oil on Sauté. Add fish and sear for 1 minute on each side. Add the rest of the ingredients and cover. Cook on High for 8 minutes. Open and serve.

Trout and Capers Sauce

Cook time: 12 minutes| Serves: 4| Per serving: Calories 200; Carbs 6g; Fat 12g; Protein 9g

Ingredients:

- Trout fillets – 4, boneless
- Cherry tomatoes – 1 cup, halved
- Garlic – 2 cloves, minced
- Capers – 2 tbsps. drained and chopped
- Salt and pepper to taste
- Parsley – 1 tbsp. chopped
- Oil – 1 tbsp.
- Veggie stock - ½ cup

Directions:

Heat oil on Sauté. Add garlic, capers, salt and pepper and cook for 2 minutes. Add the rest of the ingredients and cover. Cook on High for 10 minutes. Serve.

Lemon Cod and Scallions

Cook time: 12 minutes| Serves: 4 | Per serving: Calories 200; Carbs 6g ; Fat 12g; Protein 8g

Ingredients:

- Cod fillets – 4, boneless
- Zest of 1 lemon, grated
- Juice of ½ lemon
- Scallions – 4, chopped
- White wine vinegar – 1 tsp.
- Chicken stock – 1 cup
- Parsley – ¼ cup, chopped

- Salt and pepper to taste

Directions:

Combine everything in the Pot. Cover and cook on High for 12 minutes. Serve.

Cod and Cauliflower Rice
Cook time: 12 minutes| Serves: 4| Per serving: Calories 232; Carbs 6g; Fat 9g; Protein 8g

Ingredients:

- Cod filets – 4, boneless
- Salt and pepper to taste
- Cauliflower – 1 cup, riced
- Chicken stock – 1 cup
- Tomato puree – 2 tbsps.
- Cilantro - 1 tbsp. chopped

Directions:

Combine everything in the pot and cover. Cook on High for 12 minutes. Serve.

Spicy Trout
Cook time: 12 minutes | Serves: 4| Per serving: Calories 200; Carbs 6g; Fat 12g; Protein 9g

Ingredients:

- Trout fillets – 4 boneless
- Chili pepper – 2 tbsps. minced
- Juice of 1 lime
- Veggie stock – ½ cup
- Salt and pepper to taste
- Cayenne pepper to taste
- Chives – 1 tbsp. chopped, for garnish

Directions:

Add everything in the pot, except the chives. Cover and cook on High for 10 minutes. Sprinkle with chives and serve.

Salmon Cakes and Sauce
Cook time: 15 minutes | Serves: 4| Per serving: Calories 192; Carbs 8g; Fat 9g; Protein 7g

Ingredients:

- Oil – 1 tsp.
- Egg – 1, whisked
- Salmon meat – 1 pound, minced
- Lemon zest – 2 tbsps. grated
- Lemon juice – 1 tsp.
- Salt and pepper to taste

- Tomato sauce – 1 cup

Directions:

In a bowl, combine everything except the tomato sauce and oil. Mix and make cakes out of this mix. Heat oil on Sauté and cook the cakes 2 minutes per side. Add tomato sauce and cover. Cook on High for 8 minutes. Serve.

Cod and Strawberries Sauce

Cook time: 15 minutes| Serves: 4| Per serving: Calories 200; Carbs 5g; Fat 10g; Protein 9g

Ingredients:

- Cod fillets – 6, boneless
- Olive oil – 2 tbsps.
- Shallots – 2, minced
- Garlic – 2 cloves, minced
- Parsley – 2 tbsps. chopped
- Strawberries – 1 cup, chopped
- Lemon juice – 2 tbsps.
- Salt and pepper to taste
- Balsamic vinegar – 2 tbsps.

Directions:

Heat oil on Sauté. Add the shallots and garlic and cook for 2 minutes. Add the vinegar, berries, salt and pepper and cook for 2 minutes more. Add the fish and cover and cook on High for 10 minutes. Open, sprinkle with parsley and drizzle with lemon juice. Serve.

Chapter 11 Desserts

Mint Chocolate Chip Ice Cream

Cook time: 5 minutes |Serves: 6| Per serving: Calories 351; Carbs 6.8 g; Fat 31.4g; Protein 8.8g

Ingredients:

- Egg whites – 6
- Vanilla extract – 4 tsps.
- Mint extract – 1 tsp.
- Swerve, confectioners – ½ cup
- Slivered almonds – ¼ cup
- Shredded coconut – ¼ cup
- Heavy whipping cream – 2 and 2/3 cups
- Sugar-free chocolate chips – ½ cup

Directions:

Beat egg whites until stiff peaks form. Gently fold in whipping cream, coconut, almond, swerve, mint, and vanilla. Mix thoroughly. Cover and freeze for 2 to 4 hours. Before serving, press Sauté on the Instant Pot. Add the chocolate chips and continue to stir until melts. Do not burn. Press Cancel and remove melted chocolate. Scoop ice cream on serving bowls. Drizzle with melted chocolate and serve.

Ice Cream Bites

Cook time: 5 minutes| Serves: 7| Per serving: Calories 170; Carbs 5.7g; Fat 16g; Protein 2.1g

Ingredients:

- Sugar-free chocolate chips – 6 tbsps.
- Full-fat cream cheese – 4 ounces, softened
- Full-fat coconut milk – ½ cup
- Heavy whipping cream – 1 cup
- Swerve, confectioners – ½ cup
- Vanilla extract – ½ tsp.

Directions:

Add 1 cup of water into the Instant Pot and insert the trivet. In a bowl, combine vanilla, swerve, whipping cream, coconut milk, cream cheese, and chocolate chips. Mix well and drop onto greased egg bites molds. Place molds on top of the trivet and cover loosely with foil. Close the lid and press Manual. Cook 5 minutes on High. Do a natural pressure release. Remove the molds and freeze for at least 1 hour. Serve.

Mini Chocolate Cakes

Cook time: 20 minutes| Serves: 4| Per serving: Calories 158; Carbs 9 g; Fat 11.5g; Protein 5.1g

Ingredients:

- Almond flour – 1 cup
- Egg- 1
- Sugar-free chocolate chips – ½ cup
- Baking soda – ¼ tsp.
- Unsweetened cocoa powder – ¼ cup
- Water – 1 cup

Directions:

Add 1-cup water into the Instant Pot and add in the trivet. In a bowl, add cocoa powder, baking soda, chocolate chips, almond flour, and egg. Mix with a hand mixer. Add the batter into 4 greased ramekins. Cover with foil and place on top of the trivet. Close the lid and press Manual. Cook for 20 minutes on High. Do a quick release and remove the ramekins. Serve.

Classic Brownies

Cook time: 40 minutes| Serves: 5 | Per serving: Calories 162; Carbs 8.9g; Fat 14.3g; Protein 5g

Ingredients:

- Sugar-free chocolate chips – 8 tbsps.
- Unsweetened cocoa powder – 3 tbsps.
- Butter – 2 tbsps. softened
- Chopped walnuts – ½ cup
- Egg – 1
- Swerve – ½ cup
- Almond flour – 1 cup
- Salt – ½ tsp.
- Vanilla extract – ½ tsp.

Directions:

Pour 1 cup water into the Instant Pot and place in the trivet. In a bowl, combine vanilla extract, salt, almond flour, swerve, egg, walnuts, butter, cocoa powder, and chocolate chips. Blend with a hand mixer and transfer the mixture into a greased dish. Place the dish onto the trivet and cover with foil. Close the lid and press Manual. Cook 40 minutes on High. Do a natural release and open. Remove, cool, slice and serve.

Easy Pecan Cookie Bars

Cook time: 40 minutes |Serves: 6| Per serving: Calories 147; Carbs 1.6g; Fat 15.6g; Protein 1.4g

Ingredients:

- Almond flour – 1 cup
- Butter – 2 tbsps. softened
- Swerve – ½ cup
- Chopped pecans – ½ cup
- Vanilla extract – ½ tsp.
- Cinnamon – ½ tsp. ground
- Nutmeg – ½ tsp. ground
- Baking soda – ¼ tsp.
- Water - 1 cup for the pot

Directions:

Mix butter and flour in a bowl. Add baking soda, nutmeg, cinnamon, vanilla, pecans, and swerve. Mix to make a dough. Add 1-cup water into the Instant Pot and place the trivet. Place the dough into a greased dish and place the dish on the trivet. Cover with the foil and close the lid. Press Manual and cook 40 minutes on High. Do a natural release. Open and cool. Cut into bars and serve.

Coconut Cookie Bites

Cook time: 20 minutes| Serves: 6| Per serving: Calories 129; Carbs 3.1g; Fat 11.9g; Protein 3.5g

Ingredients:

- Butter – 2 tbsps. softened
- Eggs – 2
- Almond flour – 1 cup
- Unsweetened coconut flakes – ¾ cup
- Swerve, - ½ cup
- Almond butter – ½ cup, smooth
- Baking powder – ½ tsp.
- Vanilla extract – ½ tsp.
- Salt – ½ tsp.
- Water – 1 cup for the pot

Directions:

In a bowl, mix together salt, vanilla, baking powder, almond butter, swerve, coconut, almond flour, eggs, and butter. Mix well. Add 1 cup water into the Instant Pot and place in the trivet. Transfer the mixture into a greased egg bites pan. Place the dish onto the trivet and cover with foil. Work in batches if necessary. Close the lid and press Manual. Cook for 20 minutes on High. Do a natural release. Open and remove, serve.

Pound Cake

Cook time: 40 minutes| Serves: 8| Per serving: Calories 213; Carbs 2.1g; Fat 20.2g; Protein 6.5g

Ingredients:

- Eggs – 3
- Almond flour – 1 cup
- Swerve – 2/3 cups
- Heavy cream – ¼ cup
- Full-fat cream cheese – 4 ounces, softened
- Butter – 2 tbsps. softened
- Baking powder – ½ tsp.
- Vanilla extract – ½ tsp.
- Salt – ½ tsp.
- Water – 1 cup for the pot

Directions:

In a bowl, whisk together the heavy cream, swerve, flour, and eggs. Stir in salt, vanilla, baking powder, butter, and cream cheese. Mix well. Add 1 cup water into the Instant Pot and place in the trivet. Transfer the mixture into a greased dish and cover with a foil. Place the bowl on top of the trivet. Close the lid and press Manual. Cook for 40 minutes on High. Do a natural release. Open and remove. Remove the foil. Cook in the oven at 350F for 2 to 5 minutes to brown the top. Cool, slice and serve.

Chocolate Brownies

Cook time: 20 minutes |Serves: 8 | Per serving: Calories 180; Carbs 2.4g; Fat 17.5g; Protein 4.8g

Ingredients:

- Cocoa powder – ½ cup, unsweetened
- Unsweetened dark chocolate chunks – ¼ cup
- Cream cheese – 1 cup
- Large eggs – 2
- Coconut oil – 3 tbsps.
- Salt – ½ tsp.
- Swerve – ¾ cup
- Water – 1 cup for the pot

Directions:

In a bowl, combine the coconut oil, eggs, and cream cheese. Beat thoroughly until smooth. Add dark chocolate chunks, swerve, salt and cocoa powder. Beat until mixed thoroughly. Grease a cake pan with some oil and line with parchment paper. Dust the paper with some cocoa powder and pour in the butter. Flatten the surface and loosely cover with aluminum foil. Add 1 cup of water in the Instant Pot. Set the steam rack at the bottom of the steel insert and place the cake pan on top.

Seal the lid and press Manual. Cook for 20 minutes. When done, release the pressure naturally. Open the lid and remove the pan. Cool and serve.

Almond Butter Cookies

Cook time: 25 minutes| Serves: 15| Per serving: Calories 154; Carbs 1.5g; Fat 15.3g; Protein 2.9g

Ingredients:

- Almond flour – 1 ½ cup
- Coconut flour – ½ cup
- Eggs – 3
- Coconut oil – ¾ cup, melted
- Almond butter – 3 tbsp.
- Cocoa powder – ¼ cup, unsweetened
- Swerve – ½ cup
- Salt – ½ tsp.
- Water – 1 cup for the pot

Directions:

Add 1-cup water in the Instant Pot and place in the trivet. Line a round baking pan with parchment paper and set aside. In a bowl, add coconut flour, almond flour, swerve, cocoa butter, salt, and mix. Add almond butter, coconut oil, and eggs. Beat on high speed until fully mixed. Scoop out 15 cookies and place them in the prepared baking pan. Place the pan in the pot and cover with aluminum foil. Seal and cook for 25 minutes. When done, release the pressure naturally. Open the lid and remove the pan. Cool and serve.

Eggnog

Cook time: 10 minutes| Serves: 4| Per serving: Calories 437; Carbs 5.3 g; Fat 41.7g; Protein 9.5g

Ingredients:

- Unsweetened almond milk – 3 cups
- Egg yolks – 10
- Swerve – 1 cup
- Whipped cream – 3 cups
- Vanilla extract – 1 tsp.
- Rum extract – 2 tsps.
- Ground cinnamon – ½ tsp.

Directions:

Press Sauté and add the almond milk, cinnamon and vanilla extract. Stir well and cook for 5 to 6 minutes. Meanwhile, place egg yolks in a deep bowl. Add one cup of swerve and stir well. Pour the mixture into the Instant Pot and mix well. Continue to cook for 2 minutes more. Stir in the rum extract and whipped cream. Gently simmer for 2 to 3 minutes and press Cancel. Transfer the eggnog to serving glasses and chill. Refrigerate for 1 hour before serving.

Cherry Pudding
Cook time: 6 minutes| Serves: 5| Per serving: Calories 153; Carbs 2g; Fat 14.2g; Protein 4.5g

Ingredients:

- Whipped cream – ¾ cup
- Almond milk – ¾ cup, unsweetened
- Egg whites – 4
- Powdered stevia – 3 tsps.
- Cherry extract – 1 tsp. sugar-free
- Xanthan gum – ¼ tsp.
- Water – 2 cups for the pot

Directions:

In a bowl, combine egg whites, almond milk, and heavy cream. Beat thoroughly on high for 3 minutes. Pour the mixture into 5 ramekins. Add 2 cups of water into the Instant Pot. Position a trivet at the bottom and place the ramekins on top. Lock and cook 3 minutes on High. When done, press Cancel and release the pressure naturally. Open the pot and cool. Refrigerate for 1 hour before serving.

Chocolate Bundt Cake
Cook time: 20 minutes| Serves: 10| Per serving: Calories 137; Carbs 1.9g; Fat 12.9g; Protein 4.6g

Ingredients:

- Almond flour – 1 cup
- Cocoa powder – ½ cup, unsweetened
- Walnuts – 3 tbsps.
- Large eggs – 4
- Coconut oil – 4 tbsps. melted
- Heavy cream – ½ cup
- Baking powder – 1 tsp.
- Powdered stevia – 1 tsp.
- Water – 2 cups for the pot

Directions:

Combine all dry ingredients in a bowl. Mix well and then add coconut oil, eggs, and heavy cream. Beat until well combined. Grease a bundt pan with cooking spray. Pour in the batter and set aside. Add 2 cups of water in the Instant Pot. Position a trivet and place in the bundt pan on top. Lock and cook 20 minutes on High. When done, press Cancel and release pressure naturally. Open the pot and remove. Cool, slice and serve.

Strawberry Cake

Cook time: 20 minutes | Serves: 6 | Per serving: Calories 195; Carbs 4.2g; Fat 16.4g; Protein 5.7g

Ingredients:

- Almond flour – 2 cups
- Coconut flour – 1 cup
- Unsweetened cocoa powder – ¼ cup
- Baking soda – 1 tsp.
- Baking powder – ½ tsp.
- Salt – ½ tsp.
- Unsweetened almond milk – 1 cup
- Eggs – 3
- Egg whites – 2
- Whipped cream – 3 cups, sugar-free
- Stevia extract – 1 tsp.
- Strawberry extract – 2 tsps.
- Water – 1 cup

Directions:

Line springform pan with parchment paper and set aside. Combine the coconut flour, almond flour, cocoa powder, baking soda, baking powder, and salt in a mixing bowl. Mix well and gradually add milk. With a hand mixer, beat on high speed. One at a time, add the eggs and beat constantly. Finally, add the egg whites and mix well. Transfer the batter to the prepared springform pan and flatten the surface with a spatula. Cover loosely with some aluminum foil. Add 1-cup water in the Instant Pot. Place the trivet in the pot and gently place the springform on top. Cover and press Manual. Cook 20 minutes. Open and carefully remove the pan. Place on a wire rack and cool. Meanwhile, place stevia, whipped cream, and strawberry extract in a bowl. Beat with a hand mixer to combine well. Pour the mixture over the chilled crust and refrigerate for 1 hour before use.

Creamy Raspberry Cake

Cook time: 10 minutes | Serves: 8 | Per serving: Calories 222; Carbs 5.3g; Fat 18.3g; Protein 3.9g

Ingredients:

- Coconut flour – ½ cup
- Heavy cream – ¼ cup
- Fresh raspberries – ½ cup
- Egg yolks – 5
- Butter - ¼ cup
- Powdered stevia – 3 tsps.
- Baking powder – 1 tsp.
- Vanilla extract – 1 tsp. sugar-free
- Coconut oil – ¼ cup

- Water – 2 cups for the pot

Directions:

Except for raspberries, combine all dry ingredients in a bowl and mix well. Add all wet ingredients and beat unit fully combined. Line springform pan with some parchment paper and pour in the batter. Spread the raspberries on top by tucking them into the batter. Pour in 2 cups of water in the IP. Position a trivet in the pot and place the pan on top. Secure the lid cook 10 minutes on High. When done, press Cancel and do a quick release. Open the pot and let it chill before serving.

Ruby Pears
Cook time: 10 minutes| Serves: 4| Per serving: Calories 145; Carbs 12g; Fat 5.6g; Protein 12g

Ingredients:

- Pears – 4
- Juice and zest of 1 lemon
- Grape juice – 26 ounces
- Currant jelly – 11 ounces
- Garlic – 4 cloves, peeled
- Vanilla bean – ½
- Peppercorns – 4
- Rosemary sprigs – 2

Directions:

Pour the jelly and grape juice into the Instant Pot and mix with lemon zest and lemon juice. Dip each pear in this mix. Wrap them in aluminum foil and arrange them in the steamer basket of the Instant Pot. Add the garlic cloves, peppercorns, rosemary, and vanilla bean to the juice mixture. Place the steamer basket in the Instant Pot and cover the pot. Cook on High for 10 minutes. Take the pears out, unwrap them, and arrange them on plates. Serve cold with cooking juice poured on top.

Lemon Marmalade
Cook time: 16 minutes| Serves: 8| Per serving: Calories 458; Carbs 124g; Fat 1g; Protein 1.3g

Ingredients:

- Lemons – 2 pounds, washed, peeled, sliced and cut into quarters
- Sugar – 2 pounds
- Water – 2 cups

Directions:

Put the lemon pieces into the Instant Pot. Add water, cover, and cook on High for 10 minutes. Do a natural release and open. Add the sugar and mix. Cook and stir for 6 minutes on Sauté. Serve.

Berry Jam

Cook time: 20 minutes| Serves: 12| Per serving: Calories 331; Carbs 85g; Fat 0g; Protein 0g

Ingredients:

- Cranberries – 1 pound
- Strawberries – 1 pound
- Blueberries – ½ pound
- Blackcurrant – ¼ pound
- Sugar – 2 pounds
- Zest from 1 lemon
- Salt to taste
- Water – 2 tbsps.

Directions:

In the Instant Pot, mix all the berries, blackcurrants, lemon zest, and sugar. Stir and set aside for 1 hour. Add salt and water. Mix well. Press Sauté and bring the mixture to a boil. Then cover and cook 10 minutes on High. Do a natural release and open. Bring to a boil again and simmer for 4 minutes. Serve.

Pear Jam

Cook time: 4 minutes| Serves: 12| Per serving: Calories 90; Carbs 20g; Fat 0g; Protein 0g

Ingredients:

- Pears – 8, cored and cut into quarters
- Apples – 2, peeled, cored and cut into quarters
- Apple juice – ¼ cup
- Cinnamon – 1 tsp. ground

Directions:

In the Instant Pot, mix the pears with apples, cinnamon, and apple juice and stir. Cover the pot and cook on High for 4 minutes. Do a natural release and open. Blend with a hand mixer, cool, and serve.

Carrot Cake II

Cook time: 32 minutes| Serves: 6| Per serving: Calories 140; Carbs 23.4g; Fat 3.5g; Protein 4.3g

Ingredients:

- Flour – 5 ounces
- Salt to taste
- Baking powder – ¾ tsp.
- Baking soda – ½ tsp.
- Ground cinnamon – ½ tsp.

- Nutmeg – ¼ tsp.
- Allspice – ½ tsp.
- Egg – 1
- Yogurt – 3 tbsps.
- Sugar – ½ cup
- Pineapple juice – ¼ cup
- Olive oil – 4 tbsps.
- Carrots – 1/3 cup, peeled and grated
- Pecans – 1/3 cup, toasted and chopped
- Coconut flakes – 1/3 cup
- Cooking spray
- Water – 2 cups

Directions:

In a bowl, mix the flour with baking soda, baking powder, salt, allspice, cinnamon, and nutmeg and mix. In another bowl, mix the egg with yogurt, sugar, pineapple juice, oil, carrots, pecans, and coconut flakes and mix thoroughly. Combine the two mixtures and stir well. Pour this into a springform cake tin greased with cooking spray. Add water to the Instant Pot, then place a steamer basket. Place the springform tin on top of the steamer basket and cover the Instant Pot. Cook on High for 32 minutes. Do a natural release and open. Cool, slice, and serve.

Raisin Pudding

Cook time: 20 minutes| Serves: 4| Per serving: Calories 404; Carbs 89.8 g; Fat 1g; Protein 3.6g

Ingredients:

- Raisins – 3 cups
- Rum – ½ cup
- Sugar – 1 tbsp.
- Cocoa powder – 1 tbsp.

Directions:

Cover everything in the Instant Pot and cover with the lid. Cook on Low for 20 minutes. Do a natural release. Serve.

Conclusion

The Instant Pot can assist you in adding variety and ease to your meal preparation. You can eat healthily and enjoy juicy meals that are perfectly cooked in a short time. As you have noticed, this book is suitable for both beginner and experienced cooks and has a wide variety of recipes for any taste. This Instant Pot cookbook is a must-have for every family. Recipes are created in a clear and understandable manner, and ingredients are easy to find. With this Instant Pot cookbook, you will cook much better, tastier, and faster meals for yourself and your family.

Printed in Great Britain
by Amazon

21546311R00079